CONTENTS

1. Introduction

Gatsby's world of indulgence and excess, set against a recent history of mindless war, seems to be just as appropriate now as in 1925. Our somewhat heroic, somewhat feeble Jay Gatsby has continued to capture the imagination of the readers of 'The Great Gatsby'. The book continues to sell, and movie adaptations continue to be watched, and tickets to 1920s style Gatsby parties are sold year in, year out. The Leonardo Di Caprio meme will be used again and again. Gatsby prevails.

In this guide, I'm going to be looking at the background that shaped the story, as well as the language and structure of the novel. In addition to this, I'm going to look at a few example exam questions and provide answers to them. I hope you find it useful!

Many thanks to lovely Anna Reynard for all your help and excellent Gatsby knowledge.

Grainne Hallahan

2. Chapter Summaries

Chapter One

The story opens with our narrator, Nick Carraway, reminiscing on some advice his father gave him: "Whenever you feel like criticising anyone...just remember that all the people in the world haven't had the advantages you have." This reflective tone continues as Carraway looks back over his time in the east, and refers to the book he is writing about a man called Gatsby who 'turned out all right in the end'.

Carraway explains to the reader that after the Great War he decided to go into the bond business, and moved out East. He moved to New York, and explains the unique and strange location of the novel: the East Egg and the West Egg. Carraway lives in an 'eyesore' on the West Egg, the less fashionable of the two eggs, next door to a mansion.

Nick goes to visit his cousin, Daisy, and her husband Tom Buchanan. They have just moved into a house on the East Egg. Whilst there, Nick is introduced to Jordan Baker, a young woman who is a friend of Daisy, and whose face he recognises; Jordan mentions that she knows his neighbour, Gatsby. The visit is fraught with tension: Tom has recently read a book called 'The Rise of the Colonial Empires' and is ranting about the threats to the nordic race; during dinner Tom receives a phone call and Jordan informs Nick that Tom is having an affair; Daisy confesses to Nick that she has "had a very bad time" and "feels pretty cynical about everything".

As the evening ends, Nick realises where he knows Jordan from- she is a famous golfer who was recently accused of cheating. As he is leaving, Daisy and Tom ask him about the girl he was engaged to back home. Nick denies this, and tells the reader that it was the reason he left- so as not to be 'rumoured into marriage'.

When he arrives home, Nick sees his neighbour Gatsby in his garden, and notices that he is looking at a green light. Then Nick realises he is all alone, and Gatsby has vanished.

Chapter Two

This chapter mainly centres around Tom's mistress, Myrtle. Nick describes the 'valley of ashes', a space between the West Egg and New York, grey from 'impenetrable cloud', with farm land, 'grotesque gardens', a railroad, and a river that serves barges. Above the valley is an advert for a long-gone optician, two hovering eyes with spectacles: Doctor T.J. Eckleberg.

Nick has heard about Tom's mistress from several people now, and notes that she is 'resented' amongst his acquaintances. Tom forces Nick to meet his mistress by taking him to the garage where her husband, George works. Tom is selling George his car, and they exchange terse words that reveal Tom's power over George. George's wife, Myrtle, then appears. Nick describes her as "thickish" and comments that "her face...contained no gleam of beauty" but concedes she is "smouldering".

When George is out of earshot, Tom commands Myrtle to catch the net train to New York. They travel up in separate cars, and once they arrive Myrtle buys a copy of 'Town Tattle', and a puppy from a seller on the street. Nick tries to excuse himself, but again is forced to stay. They go to 'the apartment', and Tom takes a bottle of whisky from a locked bureau. Together they get drunk, and for Nick this is only the second time in his life he has been drunk. Nick leaves to buy cigarettes, but when he returns Tom and Myrtle have 'disappeared', he sits waiting and they reappear, and then guests arrive.

Catherine, Myrtle's sister, and Mr and Mrs Mckee arrive, and the party starts. Myrtle changes into a different dress, and begins to behave more outrageously. Mr Mckee is a photographer, and his work is discussed. Catherine speaks to Nick alone, and tells him that she went to a party at Gatsby's recently- and comments that she believes Gatsby is the nephew of Kaiser Wilhelm. Catherine also tells Nick that Tom's wife is catholic and refuses to divorce him- and Nick is shocked at the 'elaborateness of the lie'.

Nick keeps trying but failing to leave. Myrtle tells Nick about the day she met Tom and their affair began. The party continues with people falling asleep, leaving, returning, and then at midnight Tom and Myrtle fight over whether Myrtle has 'any right to mention Daisy's name', and Tom breaks her nose.

At this point Nick leaves with Mr Mckee. He remembers standing by Mr McKee's bed, with Mr McKee inside the covers in his underwear, looking through photographs, and then lying half asleep at Pennsylvania Station, waiting for the train.

Chapter Three

This chapter opens with a description of the indulgent and flamboyant parties Gatsby has been holding, and Nick has been observing over the summer. Nick describes the first night he went to the party, taking pains to point out that he was invited, unlike many of the others who turn up and treat it like an 'amusement park'.

When Nick arrives feeling uneasy, and tries unsuccessfully to find Gatsby. He then spots Jordan Baker, and attaches himself to her. They mix with other guests and Nick hears theories as to Gatsby's past: he killed a man, he was a German spy. Jordan and Nick happen across the man with owl spectacles in the library. He has been drunk for a week and tells Nick and Jordan how impressed he is that the books are not fake, but notes that the pages have not been cut. The pair leave and watch the dancing in the garden. Champagne is being handed out in glasses the size of finger bowls.

Then there is a 'significant, elemental, and profound' change. A man smiles at Nick, and tells him he recognises him from the war. They discuss places in France they both went to, and Nick starts to enjoy himself. Nick confides in the stranger that this is an 'unusual' party for him, as he has not met the host. The man is confused, and then tells him that HE is Gatsby. Nick is both embarrassed, but also in awe of Gatsby, and his smile of 'eternal reassurance'. Then a butler calls Gatsby away.

Jordan tells Nick that Gatsby told her he went to Oxford, but she doesn't believe it. Together they watch a Jazz band play, and Nick observes Gatsby, standing apart from his guests: sober and separate. Gatsby asks to speak to Jordan privately. The party continues and now people are drunk, crying and fighting. Nick goes to leave and sees Jordan, who tells him she has just heard an 'amazing thing' and asks Nick to telephone her at her aunt's house. Nick apologises to Gatsby again, and Gatsby invites him over the next morning. As Nick leaves there is a car crash in the drive, and Nick recognises one of the drivers as the owl man from the library. The crash is ridiculous, and the men far too drunk to operate a car.

Nick reflects on what he was written so far, and impresses upon the reader that these were not the only three events of his summer. He was working, seeing a girl from his office, and enjoying New York. After this party he didn't see Jordan for a while, and then they spent some time together and he begun to fall in love with her, but knew he would have to completely break things off with a girl back West, as he was 'one of the few honest people that [he has] ever known'.

Chapter Four

Nick opens with a list of people who have been attending Gatsby's parties over the summer- it is a mixture of people from the East and West Egg, all attached to scandal and outrageous behaviour. One morning Gatsby appears outside Nick's house in his flamboyant cream car, and invites him to lunch in the city. As they drive in, Nick considers how Gatsby has not lived up to his initial expectations when they first met at the party, and now he considers him just the man who lives in a big house next door. Gatsby suddenly asks Nick what he thinks of him, and Nick tries to evade the question. Gatsby then interrupts him, and tells him he wants to tell him something about himself, so that Nick knows the truth and can ignore the stories that people tell about him. Nick listens sceptically as Gatsby tells him he comes from the mid-west, and his dead wealthy parents had sent him to Oxford, and he had then gone to Europe, before fighting in the war. It is only when Gatsby shows him a medal and a photograph of himself at Oxford that Nick considers that this might all be true. Gatsby then mysteriously tells Nick that this was all so that when he sees Jordan later, she can tell him something important, and that he wanted Nick to know he was 'somebody'. Nick is annoyed by the mystery, but goes along with it.

They go for lunch with Mr Wolfsheim, and Mr Wolfsheim tells Nick a story about his friend who was shot at the restaurant opposite. After Mr Wolfsheim mistakes Nick for a man looking for a 'business connection', Gatsby goes to make some phone calls, and Mr Wolfsheim tells Nick how Gatsby is a fine 'Oggsford' man, and asks Nick if he knows about 'Oggsford'. When Gatsby returns they finish lunch and Mr Wolfsheim leaves; to Nick's amazement, Gatsby then tells Nick that Wolfsheim was the man who fixed the 1919 World Series. Nick then sees Tom, but when he goes to introduce Tom to Gatsby, Gatsby has vanished.

Later, Jordan tells Nick of the time she and Daisy became friends when they were young women during the war. Jordan recalls seeing Daisy and a young officer called Gatsby in a car, and that the officer looked at Daisy 'in a way that every young girl wants to be looked at sometime'. Jordan doesn't see this officer again, and Daisy goes on to get engaged to Tom. The day before the wedding, Jordan finds her drunk and holding a letter she won't let Jordan see, and destroys it. She tells Jordan to tell everyone that she's changed her mind. Daisy sobers up, and the next day marries Tom. Jordan thought Daisy loved Tom as she was always so preoccupied about where he was, but that same year Tom was in a car crash with a hotel chamber maid in his passenger seat. The next year Daisy had a baby, and they move around a lot. It was only when Daisy heard Jordan asking about Gatsby, and Daisy asked Jordan "What Gatsby?" that Jordan realised it was the same one. Nick remarks that this is coincidence, and Jordan insists that it isn't, and that Gatsby bought that house to be close to Daisy. Now Nick sees Gatsby differently. Jordan tells

Nick that Gatsby has requested that Nick invite Daisy for tea at his house, so that Gatsby can come and see her- but Nick is not to tell Daisy that Gatsby will be there. It must be Nick's house so that Daisy can see Gatsby's house from there.

Nick and Jordan then embrace.

Chapter Five

Nick returns home to see Gatsby's home lit from 'tower to cellar', and soon a clearly uneasy Gatsby arrives asking Nick to come out with him, but Nick declines, and tells him he has spoken to Jordan and has agreed to the plan. Gatsby worries about the cutting of his grass (and Nick suspects he means the cutting of Nick's grass), and then offers Nick a deal to help him make money- again, Nick declines.

Nick is happy, and sleeps well. The next day he calls Jordan and invites her to tea- telling her to not bring Tom, to which she readily agrees.

The following day, a man arrives to cut the grass, and then another man brings a whole 'greenhouse' of flowers. Gatsby arrives looking as if he hasn't slept, and agitated. Nick is unsuccessful in his attempts to calm him down, and before it is even four pm (the traditional time for tea) Gatsby wants to leave- just at that moment, Daisy arrives. Daisy and Nick greet each other warmly, and share a joke, but when they walk into the living room, Gatsby has gone. Confused, Nick then answers the knock at the door, and there is Gatsby, soaking wet from the rain and 'glaring tragically' at Nick. Gatsby and Daisy then awkwardly greet each other, and Gatsby is painfully tense- at one point almost smashing a clock from the mantelpiece. Nick leaves the room to try and give them some privacy, but Gatsby follows him- crestfallen and ready to give up. At this point, Nick loses his patience and tells Gatsby he needs to stop 'acting like a little boy' and reprimands him for being 'rude'. Nick then leaves the pair alone, and wanders outside, looking at Gatsby's house.

After a while, Nick returns to find the couple quite transformed and the embarrassment gone. Daisy has been crying, and Gatsby is 'glowing'. He now greets Nick warmly, and invites both Nick and Daisy over to his house. Nick describes the journey over to Gatsby's mansion, and the opulent rooms with admiration and sees it all with echoes of his experience there as a party goer. They stop to have a drink of Chartreuse, and then go to Gatsby's bedroom- which is the plainest of all the rooms. Daisy is enthralled with Gatsby's shirts, and cries at how beautiful they are.

They then move outside to see the gardens, swimming pool, and hydroplane. There, Gatsby tells Daisy about the green light on her dock, and Nick observes that now for Gatsby that 'the colossal significance of that light vanished forever'.

Back inside, Nick notices a photo of Gatsby with a man, who Gatsby tells him is Dan Cody, and that he was his best friend, though he has now died. Gatsby is then called away to an ominous sounding phone call, and then Daisy calls him back to look at the pink clouds that have filled the sky following the storm. They call for Gatsby's 'boarder' Mr Klipspringer to play the piano- he is reluctant, but Gatsby insists.

Nick considers how important this moment is to Gatsby, and how everything in his life for the past five years has been building to this. He then leaves them both in the house together.

Chapter Six

Gatsby is disturbed at home when a reporter calls and asks him for a 'statement'. The reporter was acting on a hunch based on the gossip that had arisen as a consequence of Gatsby's parties. The 'underground pipe line to Canada' (not a real pipe line- but part of a legend explaining how alcohol came into the US) was being linked to Gatsby, and other outlandish ideas.

Nick retells the story that Gatsby apparently told him 'some time later' when Nick believed 'everything and nothing' that he heard about Gatsby. James Gatz was the legal name of Gatsby, but he changed it at 17 after he saw Dan Cody's yacht on Lake Superior. It is James Gatz spotted it, but a newly created Jay Gatsby rowed out to give him sailing advice.

Nick supposes that Gatsby had the name ready- his parents had been farm people, and in Gatsby's mind he saw himself as an immaculate conception. Nick believes Gatsby was the 'son of god', and that his father's business was services to a valueless beauty. The Jay Gatsby that James Gatz invented was the stuff of seventeen-year-old boys' dreams- and he remained that way until the end.

For a year James Gatz had been on the lake doing manual jobs, working from hand to mouth. He had encounters with women, but was contemptuous of them. The virgins for their ignorance, and the others for their hysteria. Privately, Gatsby spent his time tormented by dreams of wealth, whilst falling asleep in primitive lodgings. Every night his dreams became more detailed, and more consuming.

A few months earlier, Gatsby had spent two weeks at a Lutheran college, before dropping out. He was disappointed both by their apparent lack of interest in what he considered his destiny, and the janitorial work he had to do in order to pay for the course. Gatsby returned to the lake, still searching for his future, when he met Cody.

Cody had made his money in metal, and at fifty years old, he was now a millionaire several times over. His mind was softening, and women tried to separate him from his money. Ella Kaye was his 'Madame de Maintenton' (Louis XIV unofficial wife- and a huge influence on his reign) and she had sent him on this yacht trip- by the time Gatsby met him, he had been away for five years.

To Gatsby, the yacht represented all the glamour in the world. He would have smiled that winning smile, knowing people liked him when he smiles. Cody recognised that Gatsby was smart and ambitious, and took him on board and into his life. Gatsby sailed off to the Caribbean with a new wardrobe, and a vague job title. Gatsby had many roles, but primarily seemed tasked with ensuring that Dan Cody didn't behave in a way whilst drunk, that he wouldn't approve of when sober. Cody trusted Gatsby, and confided in him. For five years they sailed round America. It ended when Ella Kaye joined them, and a week later, Dan Cody died.

Nick recalls Dan Cody's portrait in Gatsby's house, and he attributes Gatsby's sobriety to Dan Cody's influence. Cody left Gatsby $25, 000, but Gatsby never received it- Ella Kaye received it instead.

Nick assures the reader he is telling this story to correct the rumours surrounding Gatsby's history.

For several weeks, Nick and Gatsby's relationship was paused whilst Nick spent his time in New York, and with Jordan, and with Jordan's aunt. One Sunday afternoon, Nick called on Gatsby, and soon after he arrived, a couple joined them, Mr and Mrs Sloane, and with them was Tom Buchanan. Gatsby was visibly uneasy in Tom's company, and an awkward conversation followed. The situation is made worse by Gatsby's lack of knowledge regarding social etiquette of the upper classes, and the visit ends with a polite but insincere invitation for Gatsby to join them for lunch, and when to their surprise Gatsby accepts, they leave without him. To expresses concern to Nick that Daisy and Gatsby know each other, and comments that women have too much freedom.

Consequently, at the party on Saturday night, Tom attends along with Daisy. Nick senses a peculiar feeling of oppressiveness, and attributes this to Tom's presence. The party had all the same components as the one he had previously attended, but this time it felt unpleasant.

Daisy and Tom are surprised that the party is full of celebrities, in particular, a beautiful actress and her director. Daisy is quite taken at first with all the famous people, but Tom less so, and he leaves them to mingle with the guests. In his absence, Daisy and Gatsby dance, and then go with Nick to sit on the steps of his home to talk for half an hour- the best part of the evening for Daisy. During dinner, Nick observes the effect of alcohol with disdain, and finds what amused him before now feels 'sceptic'.

The movie star and director remain under the plum tree, and Nick realises the director has been slowly leaning in for a kiss- and then he sees him kiss her on the cheek. Daisy approves her, but not the rest. Nick attributes her dislike in her failure to understand the simplicity that West Egg represented.

Nick waits with Daisy and Tom for their car, and Tom begins to question Gatsby's origins, and the source of his money. The couple squabble over whether it was more or less interesting than their own social circle, and Tom attempts to draw Nick into the argument. Daisy breaks off into song. Tom then insists he is going to find the truth out about Gatsby, but Daisy defends Gatsby insisting that she knows the truth, that he got the money from owning drugstores. They leave in a limousine, but before she gets in Daisy looks up at the house. Nick supposes that Daisy feels drawn back in, and must be wondering about what will happen in her absence, and be wondering if Gatsby may meet someone new who will replace her.

Nick stays late at the party at Gatsby's request, and once the guests have all either left or gone to bed, Gatsby begins to lament at Daisy's apparent lack of enjoyment, and his fear that she does not understand. Gatsby wants Daisy to tell Tom she never loved him, and for Gatsby and Daisy to go to Daisy's home in Louisville and be married. Nick warns him that 'you can't repeat the past', but Gatsby vehemently disagrees. Gatsby feels certain that it all can be fixed if he can just find the right starting place, that they could begin again.

Nick retells the first kiss between Gatsby and Daisy, and the story is full of romantic imagery and magical wonder. When they kissed, Daisy 'blossomed for him like a flower'. This stirs something inside of Nick, even though he considers the story to be full of appalling sentimentality. Gatsby's memory reminds him of something in his own past, but finds it impossible to put it into words.

Chapter Seven

One Saturday night the lights didn't come on at Gatsby's. Confused party goers arrived, and then turned their cars around and went home. Nick at first thinks Gatsby is unwell, but when he calls he discovers that he has sacked all his staff, and employed six new ones. Daisy is now visiting most afternoons and they want people who won't gossip. Nick feels this has come as a consequence of Daisy's disapproval of Gatsby's parties.

Gatsby passes on an invitation from Daisy to Nick, to come for lunch at the Buchanan's home the following day. It is the hottest day of the year, and the last hot day of the summer. Nick arrives and there is Daisy, Jordan and Gatsby there, with Tom arguing on the telephone in the other room. Jordan believes it is his 'other woman', but Nick insists it isn't, as he can hear from the conversation he is talking to George about selling his car.

Tom reenters and greets them, before leaving the room again. When he is gone, Daisy kisses Gatsby, prompting gentle teasing from Jordan, and then Daisy teases Jordan for her kisses to Nick in return. Daisy's daughter is brought in by the nurse, ad Daisy makes a fuss of her. Gatsby looks at Daisy's daughter 'with surprise'. Daisy speaks about how her daughter resembles herself, and not Nick. The daughter is shown out, and Tom returns.

The five of them drink gin, and stand looking out at Gatsby's house, before eating lunch. As they discuss what to do, Daisy expresses a desire to go into town. She complains about the heat, looks at Gatsby, and after they share a look and she says "you always look so cool". In that moment, Tom realises that she is in love with Gatsby, and with a growing anger, insists that they leave to go to town. There is tension as they get ready to leave, taking whisky and arguing about smoking.

Tom demands that Gatsby drives Tom's blue coupe, and Tom will drive Gatsby's car. Tom asks Daisy to get in with him, but Daisy ignores him and gets in with Gatsby, leaving Tom with Nick and Jordan.

Tom looks to Nick and Jordan to share his shock, but realises that they also know. Angry and embarrassed, he becomes defensive. He reveals that he has investigated Gatsby, and that he knows he didn't go to Oxford. Neither Nick nor Jordan give anything away, and Jordan gently ridicules him about his investigation. Tom is incredulous about the origins of Gatsby and Daisy's friendship.

Tom, Nick and Jordan stop to get gas at the Wilson's garage. They find George Wilson very unwell- he is asking Tom about selling the car, and the earlier telephone conversation is referenced. George reveals he needs the money to take his wife West- he has found something out and they need to leave. Tom is shaken by this realisation that Myrtle has a life apart from him. George has discovered the same thing about Myrtle, as what Tom has discovered about Daisy- and Nick notes how the two men's reactions mirror each other- and that men are the same regardless of background.

As they leave, Nick looks up and sees Myrtle at a window, and notes how she mistakes Jordan for Tom's wife when she sees the two of them sat together in Gatsby's yellow car. The three speed off to catch up with Gatsby and Daisy. When they do, they call across to each other through traffic, and after initially disagreeing, make plans to meet at the Plaza. Once there, they pay for a suite, and sit in the room, fraught with tension.

All five are on edge, and an argument quickly erupts between Daisy, Tom, and Gatsby. They hear wedding music below, and this segues the conversation into safer territory temporarily, as they discuss a fainting guest at the Buchanan's June wedding, who then outstayed his welcome at Jordan's house. This temporary reprise is ended when Tom starts grilling Gatsby on his Oxford credentials.

Gatsby tells the true story of how he went to Oxford as part of a reward after the war, but only stayed five months, so cannot truly call himself an Oxford man. Nick experiences a renewal of faith in his friend- relieved that he has told the truth.

Not swayed, Tom then directly confronts Gatsby about his relationship with Daisy, and in doing so characterises himself as the old-fashioned conservative, and Gatsby as the modern immoral.

Gatsby tells Tom the words he wanted Daisy to say: that Daisy never loved Tom, and that she wants to be with Gatsby. Tom refuses to believe it, and says it is a lie. He describes his own affairs as 'little sprees' and insists that he and Daisy love each other. At this, Daisy is furious, and begins to tell the story of what happened with Tom in Chicago- but Gatsby asks Daisy to tell Tom she never loved him. Daisy does, but as she does, Nick recognises that in her face she never really believed that she would go through with it.

Tom appeals to Daisy, and Daisy breaks, conceding that she did love Tom once. But she loves Gatsby now. Gatsby is stunned, and finds this difficult to understand. The three argue over wither Daisy is leaving Tom. Tom, desperate to win back Daisy, tells Daisy that Gatsby is involved in illegal activities, and that he is going to investigate Gatsby further. Gatsby refutes these claims, but Daisy is shocked.

Tom senses he has won, and sends Daisy home with Gatsby, confident that he has put an end to the affair. Gatsby and Daisy leave in Gatsby's car. When they're gone, Tome offers the whisky around, and Nick remembers it is his 30th birthday. Then the three of them follow in Tom's car.

The story shifts in time to an inquest, and Tom is recounting the coffee shop owner's statement regarding what has happened. He describes how he saw George Wilson unwell, he and his wife had been arguing, and then how a car came by and Myrtle ran out to it and it ran her over.

The story shifts back again, and Nick describes the car approaching the crash, and Tom is initially almost gleeful and wants to see what has happened. As they get closer he realises it is Myrtle who has been killed, and George sees them and there is confusion about the car- they realise it is Gatsby's car that hit her. No one gives Gatsby's name to the police.

They return home, and Nick refuses to go inside the Buchanan's home. As he goes to leave, he sees Gatsby in the garden. Gatsby says he is waiting to see if Daisy is okay, he is worried Tom may hurt her. Nick goes to check on her by walking round to the back of the house, and through a window he sees Daisy and Tom sitting 'intimately' in the kitchen. He senses that there is a kind of reconciliation between them. Nick tells Gatsby that all is quiet, but Gatsby insists on staying, and Nick leaves him there in the moonlight.

Chapter Eight

Nick cannot sleep, and goes over to Gatsby's, only to find he also cannot sleep. The two of them hunt for cigarettes, and Nick notes how enormous the house feels. They eventually find some, and sit and smoke. Nick urges Gatsby to leave, but Gatsby insists he must stay for Daisy. It is now Gatsby tells Nick the story of his relationship with Dan Cody (as told in chapter six). He also talks about the first time he met Daisy, and visited her house. Both Daisy's easiness with her own wealth, and her desirability to others, attracts Gatsby to Daisy. Gatsby felt his uniform gave him a cloak of invisibility, and this cloak allowed him contact now, but he knew it wouldn't always. Gatsby had let Daisy believe that he was of a similar background. They'd spent a month together before he was sent away to fight, and the two fell in love.

Gatsby did well at war and was made a captain, following armistice he was trying to get home, but was sent to Oxford by mistake. Daisy was writing and asking him to come home, but Gatsby was tied by external forces. Daisy became impatient and started dating again, and consequently met Tom. She wrote to Gatsby to tell him of the wedding, and he received the letter whilst still in Oxford.

It was now Dawn, and Gatsby begins to justify Daisy's behaviour the day before, blaming Tom. He is still struggling with the idea that Daisy ever loved Tom. Gatsby tells Nick how he tried to get back to Daisy, but it was too late and the wedding had happened. He tried to find her but was unsuccessful.

At 9am they finished breakfast. It felt like Autumn, and the gardener comes to say he will drain the pool, Gatsby tells him not to, he will swim today.

Nick eventually leaves, promising to call, and Gatsby expresses a hope Daisy will call too. Nick tells him before he goes that 'they're a rotten crowd…you're worth the whole damn bunch put together'.

At work he falls asleep, struggling to concentrate. At 12 pm Jordan telephones, and they have a tense conversation that ends with one hanging up on the other. Nick tries to call Gatsby, but he is keeping the line free for a long-distance call from Detroit.

On the train home Nick cannot look out at the ash heaps, and he hears the story being told and retold by other passengers. Nick now goes back to the previous night, and tells the story of what had happened after they left the car wreck the previous night.

Myrtle's sister Catherine arrived, drunk, and was driven to the hospital they had taken Myrtle to. George stayed at the garage, comforted by the coffee shop owner, Michaelis. Together, they discuss George's marriage, and Michaelis tries to comfort George. George shows him a dog leash he found wrapped in tissue paper, presumably a gift from her lover. Michaelis tries to reassure George, and keeps asking him about his church.

George recounts how he took Myrtle to the window and told her that 'God sees everything', with the poster of Doctor T.J. Eckleburg in the background. Eventually Wilson calms down, and Michaelis goes home to sleep, and then returns four hours later to find

George gone. Following the accounts of various witnesses, we realise that George has gone to find Gatsby.

At 2pm Gatsby put on his swimming costume, and goes to swim in the pool. Nick wonders about Gatsby's last thoughts- did he look up at the sky through the leaves of the trees and shudder at the state of the world? Although his chauffeur heard the shots, he didn't think anything of it. It wasn't until Nick arrived agitated that they realised something was amiss, and the four: Nick, the chauffeur, the gardener, and the butler, rushed down to find Gatsby dead in the pool, and Wilson dead in the gardens a little way off.

Chapter Nine

Nick is now two years past Gatsby's death and looking back on the events. He considers the days that past immediately after the murder as a stream of visits from the police, the newspapers, and from photographers. The newspaper reports were inaccurate and sensational. At the inquest, Catherine contradicted Michaelis statement and lied, saying Myrtle was faithful to her husband. The death was recorded as the actions of a man 'deranged by grief'.

In the absence of anyone else there to do it, Nick takes on the role of a sort of executor. He tries to arrange the funeral, but cannot get anyone come to pay respects to Gatsby's body that is being kept in the house. When he telephones Daisy, he discovers she and Tom have left town and are uncontactable.

Nick feels he is letting Gatsby down, and telephones Wolfsheim, but he doesn't answer. He writes to Wolfsheim. Still only police and the press call. Wolfsheim eventually writes a reply, but only to say he cannot come down and is very shocked. Nick receives one telephone call, but it is clear that it is regarding an illegal business deal, and the caller hangs up as soon as he realises he isn't speaking to Gatsby.

On the third day Gatsby's father gets in contact, and when he arrives Nick takes him to see Gatsby's dead body. Mr Gatz tells Nick he always knew his son was clever, and he believes if he had lived he would have done great things for this country.

The 'boarder' Mr Klipspringer telephones, but just wants his tennis shoes posted: he isn't interested in the funeral. Another person Nick calls implies Gatsby got what he wanted, and Nick regrets calling them- remembering they were always quick to sneer at Gatsby on the courage of his liquor.

On the morning of Gatsby's funeral, Nick goes to Wolfsheim's office to ask him to attend the funeral. At first he is refused an audience, but he insists, and eventually allowed in. Although Wolfsheim is complimentary about Gatsby, he insists he cannot come to the funeral. Disappointed, Nick returns home to get ready for the funeral.

At the house, Nick finds Mr Gatz, and he shows him a photograph Gatsby had sent him of his house- Nick notes how his father seems to believe more in the photograph than in the actual building. He tells Nick he saw Gatsby two years ago when he bought him the house he now lives in. He also shows Nick Gatsby's boyhood diary with a schedule for exercise and study inside.

No one arrives at the house for the funeral, so they wait half an hour, and then leave. Just Nick, Mr Gatz, and the few staff. At five they reach the cemetery and stop in the rain. At the graveside, the man with the owl glasses is there. He apologises for not getting to the house, and Nick tells him no one did. The Owl man says 'the poor son of a bitch'.

Nick now thinks back to his childhood journeys home from school and college, travelling West and the feeling of returning home. The thrill of pulling into the station, and the connection they felt to the country. To Nick, that is his mid-west. Not farms and prairies, but the sense of being home on returning trains. Nick now considers maybe it was a story of the West- and how he and the others were not suited for Eastern life.

Even when Nick thought of the East as exciting and superior as the West, he thought of the East as distorted. Nick considers the East as a night scene by El Greco. Disillusioned, Nick decides he must return home.

Nick doesn't want to leave without putting things in order, so he goes to see Jordan, and talks to her about his feelings about what happened between them. After he finished, she told him she was engaged to someone else. Nick doubts this story, but acts surprised. Jordan tells him it was Nick who ended it anyway, and then reminds him of a conversation they once had about driving a car- how she was wrong and that he was a 'bad driver', as in a dishonest person. Nick agrees with her, and sadly leaves.

Time passes, and when Nick sees Tom in October, he refuses to shake his hand. Nick asks Tom what he said to Wilson. Tom tells him he came to their home with a gun, and Tom told him it was Gatsby's car. He tells Nick Gatsby had it coming, and that Tom has had it bad too, and when he saw the dog biscuits in the apartment he cried. Nick realises that Tom and Daisy were careless people, and he shakes Tom's hand, considering him to be a child.

Nick goes to New York on Saturdays to avoid being at home and reminded of the parties. On his last night, Nick goes to Gatsby's house, rubs out an expletive someone had written on the steps. Nick then goes into the garden, and considers the green light, and Gatsby's obsession with the past. Nick thinks about how he was always chasing what he once had, once almost had, and hoping to obtain once again.

3. The Author

F Scott Fitzgerald was known for several things: his love affair with his wife, Zelda; his debts and alcoholism; and his extravagant lifestyle. Born in 1896 Fitzgerald in Maryland, Fitzgerald's parents were both troubled by their own problems; his family was split in two, with old money and new money and all of the associated contentions that can bring. He attended Catholic schools, and despite his poverty was surrounded by wealth. Fitzgerald's mother is often indicated as the main instigator of this pursuit of social betters- often seeking out situations for Fitzgerald to meet more wealthy friends. However, both the inequality in affluence, and Fitzgerald's inequality in the playing of sport, meant that he was always an outsider.

When he failed in sport, he wrote about it instead, and enjoyed the fame and attention of being printed in his school paper. Fitzgerald also enjoyed going to the theatre, and after being inspired by the Broadway shows he began to write his own, which were performed by drama clubs. He also formed a strong attachment to Father Sigourney Webster Fay, who he continued to keep in touch with long after he left school. Fay is thought to have nurtured Fitzgerald through his troubled childhood, and was influential on his writing- notably, *This Side of Paradise* and *The Great Gatsby.*

On leaving school, Fitzgerald was fortunate enough to be able to apply for Princeton, following the inheritance of some money. He had to take a written exam, in which he cheated, and still failed, and then an oral exam- which he passed. He was granted a place, and his first year was successful: he published many pieces of writing and fell in love. His second year was less successful: his grades fell, and his affair ended, with Fitzgerald remarking 'poor boys shouldn't dream of marrying rich girls.' Fitzgerald's academic performance was so poor he had to repeat the year, and then in 1917 World War One meant that he left Princeton to join the army, never to return to finish his studies.

It was as a freshly promoted Lieutenant that Fitzgerald first met Zelda Sayre- the woman whose love would direct the course of the rest of his life. Fitzgerald had found someone in Sayre who valued the same things as him, and together they pursued money, success and fame. The pair were engaged to marry in 1919, but Sayre made it clear that Fitzgerald would have to prove his financial prospects were respectable, and so began Fitzgerald's assault upon the publishing world.

Fitzgerald achieved a sell out success with his first shocking (and clearly autobiographical) novel *This Side of Paradise.* Overnight, Fitzgerald became a celebrity, and Fitzgerald and Sayre married in 1920 in New York. They lived a scandalous existence with the papers reporting their outrageous behaviour with gleeful shock. They dived into fountains, and undressed at theatre performances, and rode on top of taxicabs. Fitzgerald continued to have more success with short story collections and another novel- and then Zelda fell pregnant, and they left for Europe, a trip that Fitzgerald did not enjoy.

When Zelda gave birth to their daughter, she made the same announcement as the character of Daisy did in *The Great Gatsby*: 'I hope it's beautiful and a fool- a beautiful fool!' Shortly after this, Zelda reportedly had an abortion, not wanting a second child so soon after the first.

Fitzgerald's second novel, *The Beautiful and the Damned* charted the downfall of a young couple whose extravagant lifestyle drove them into damaging spending patterns, and into a pit of unhappiness. Critics were quick to point out the similarities between Anthony and Gloria Patch of the novel, and the life of the novelist and his wife.

Fitzgerald continued to write plays, short stories, and work on his novel, but was constantly getting into, and then working himself out of debt. Zelda had an affair that was described in Fitzgerald's novel *Tender is the Night* and her own *Save me the Waltz* although it is unknown the exact truth of the extra marital relationship. For Fitzgerald, another romantic dream had gone, and something between them changed forever.

On September the 20th 1924, Scott Fitzgerald wrote to his agent, Harold Ober, informing him he had finished his novel, *The Great Gatsby*. He also told him he was broke, and asked for money, despite already being in Ober's debt. They had hoped to serialise Gatsby, before releasing it as a novel, but they were unsuccessful in agreeing a deal that they were happy with. Fitzgerald was reluctant to have the novel carved up as he felt 'The Beautiful and the Damned' had been, and in the end he pinned his hopes on the novel sales and securing a movie deal.

'I feel very old this winter. I am twenty eight. I was twenty-two when I came to New York and found that you'd sold 'Head and Shoulders' to the post. I'd like to get a thrill like that again but I suppose it's only once in a lifetime.'

The Fitzgeralds moved to the French riviera became tangled up in a celebrity social circle-a mixture of actors, artists and socialites. Included in this circle was the writer Ernest Hemingway. Zelda and Scott's marriage continued to experience trouble, and Hemingway is said to have commented that Zelda was jealous of Scott's work. 1925 saw these troubles escalate: Zelda returned to ballet dancing, but following a party where a famous dancer flirted with her husband she threw herself down some stairs. Many of their social occasions ended in violence. Even when Hollywood called with the invitation to write a screenplay, the pair ended with an argument in a hotel room and Zelda burning her clothes in a bathtub.

Even with the Hollywood disaster, the couple were making more money than ever before, and yet the pair were drinking more than ever and being shut off by their friends. Hemingway's friendship with Fitzgerald had cooled, and there were arguments about the advice given over Hemingway's new novel *Farewell to Arms.*

In 1930 Zelda suffered her first mental breakdown, and her second just two years later-after which she never recovered her health and their relationship ended. Fitzgerald's novel *Tender is the Night* was published in 1934 about a couple, the woman is a mental patient, and the man a psychiatrist, and as the woman recovers, the man deteriorates. At this point, Scott's relationship with alcohol had become a real problem for him.

In 1937, Fitzgerald was able to go to Hollywood and began writing screenplays, and began a new relationship with a woman called Sheilah Graham, who worked as a hugely successful Hollywood gossip journalist.

In 1939 Fitzgerald began his last novel *The Last Tycoon*, but it was left unfinished, as he died at just forty-four of a heart attack.

4. Scott Fitzgerald and The Great Gatsby

Letters between Fitzgerald and his agent reveal a man desperate for money, and keen to maximise his financial return on his novel. There are many ways a reader can see Fitzgerald writing himself into the character of Gatsby: a man marrying out of his social class and keen to improve his own social standing to secure the love of a woman. If Fitzgerald intended us to see himself in Gatsby, he certainly didn't paint a complimentary picture. A reader could interpret Fitzgerald's decision to kill Gatsby off as a prophetic foresight that his own marriage to his Daisy would not survive the roaring twenties.

Fitzgerald was frequently caught up in scandals, and was considered to be enjoying the new found freedoms of the post-war era. Here, the parallels between the author and protagonist seem to splinter off- Gatsby threw his amazing parties, but himself never indulged in the alcohol and the implied depravity. Fitzgerald, in contrast, was never as detached- he and Zelda together lived a life that embraced the parties and reveled in the notoriety. And yet this life was punctuated with sadness, just as Gatsby's was. Fitzgerald and Zelda were known for their animosity, as much as they were for their amour.

On the tenth of April 1925, 'The Great Gatsby' was published.

Within seven years of the publication of 'The Great Gatsby' Zelda and Scott's relationship had broken down irreparably. In killing off Gatsby, and keeping the rich Buchanans together, perhaps Fitzgerald was being kind: in marrying Zelda, he had married his Daisy, and was now living out the inevitable consequence of being with someone you always feared you didn't deserve.

Structurally, choosing to re-tell the story via Nick, the autobiographical element of 'The Great Gatsby' is viewed through this prism of a storyteller who looks on at the action, rather than the Gatsby who is the hero of the story. Fitzgerald's accomplishments at college are very similar to Nick's- their success of publishing via the college newspaper, and their writing styles. Fitzgerald is simultaneously Nick and Gatsby: he is the onlooker, and the one who is looked upon. Fitzgerald lived two lives- one of anonymity in his pre-published years, and one whose every misdemeanour is recorded in gossip columns, and dissected by strangers. Those two lives are interwoven in the novel- and by electing Nick to be narrator, and survivor, we can see Fitzgerald choosing to live as his 'true' self- the unknown scholar, not the heartbroken socialite.

5. **Context**

Consumerism

Fitzgerald's notoriety with regards to spending was satirised in his self-deprecating essays 'How to live on $36,000 a year' and 'How to live on practically nothing a year'. Fitzgerald, along with the rest of the country, lived chasing debt. The West found itself unwittingly caught in a trap of consumer worship. Desire beat frugality, and many readers of 'The Great Gatsby' would recognise themselves in the characters of Myrtle, George, and Nick.

Capitalism was king, and in the United States, the 1920s saw rising salaries, the reduction of the working week from six days to five, and consequently people had more disposable income and free time to spend it: advertising stepped in. In addition to newspapers and magazines, the radio begun to cash in on the success of advertising, and people found themselves tempted by new products, vacations away, and other luxuries. Another change was the birth of brand names, and the packaging and branding of products became more important, as people begun to understand the psychology behind consumer purchases. In the novel, Fitzgerald describes Gatsby's shedding of his old name 'James Gatz' as a kind of rebranding, to appeal to a new world where his old name would be inappropriate- and his continued reinvention to appeal to one particular customer: Daisy. The one advertisement that is described in detail is, of course, Dr. T. J. Eckleburg; and it is worth noting that this advert is tattered, dilapidated and defunct. Out of date and ignored, the advert could be interpreted as a comment on the fleeting appeal of advertising, and the manner in which things that were once relevant, can quickly become irrelevant, and unfashionable.

The rise of 'gadgets' is also significant in that housework and the labour intensive tasks that previously consumed much of the working day were becoming less onerous with every advancement of technology. However, the ideal that was sold in the advertisements did not always match up to the reality, and for the working class these gadgets were out of their financial reach, and for the wealthy they still relied upon paid staff to operate these gadgets.

The Jazz Age and Prohibition

The 1920s were a curious period in history: they followed the end of the war (and all of the sadness and happiness that accompanies that) and came before the great financial crisis of the 1930s. North America's mass immigration hit a peak the decade before, in 1910, and subsequently America's culture was altered forever, with a fusion of European, African, and Asian musical cultures populating the towns and cities. Shipping had become a big business with the opening of the Panama Canal, allowing shipping between the Atlantic and the Pacific. The last notable gift of the 1910s to the 1920s was the announcement in 1919 that prohibition would start the following year: the 18th Amendment prohibiting the manufacture, sale and transportation of intoxicating liquors.

Along with prohibition came the inevitable bootlegging. Amongst others, there were rumours of an underground pipeline between the US and Canada. This 'pipeline' didn't exist in a physical sense, but rather a series of smugglers transporting the alcohol secretly, out of the prohibition free Canada, to their American counterparts. The government introduced it as part of a strategy to improve the National mood (The Anti-Saloon League argued that alcohol damaged society); practical reasons to boost the supply of barley and other grains; for religious reasons as it was believed that drinking alcohol went against God's will. Prohibition was repealed in 1933 after the Wikersham Commission report stated that Prohibition was not working. The report gave reasons of lack of agents to enforce the law, agents being bribed, the size of America making in unmanageable, lack of support from Americans, and the rise in gang crime making money out of prohibition. This lack of support of prohibition is evident throughout the novel: the casual approach to drinking populates many pages, with alcohol fueling much of the drama. However, this moral objection to alcohol manifests itself in Nick's discomfort during his second Gatsby party; the antics of the partygoers becomes 'septic' and he recounts a conversation between a young drunk woman who has had her head dunked in a swimming pool, and a doctor whose hands shake from alcohol consumption, with much disdain.

Along with the alcohol, Gatsby's parties are also full of music and dancing. The Jazz Age brought along with it the introduction to many new styles, and was a rich cultural period that shocked and excited people in America. The emergence of this new sound was an inevitability of the cultural mix following the immigration that had been happening in the decade before. It was from the African Americans that Jazz was introduced to America, but both black and white Americans were responsible for its rising popularity. Just as the radio aided the spread of advertising, it also contributed to the sharing of Jazz music, and the new technology that allowed music to be recorded enabled this new style of music to be broadcast throughout America. Fitzgerald weaves many different references to music throughout the novel- from a pianist Kilpsinger playing 'Ain't We Got Fun' to Daisy when she visits Gatsby, to the three of Nick, Daisy, and Tom sitting on Gatsby's doorstep, listening to Three O'Clock in the Morning. Along with the music, dances such as the Foxtrot and the Charleston are referenced, contributing to the impression of reckless hedonistic fun that was had at the parties. What is most notable, is when the friends stop dancing: during the confrontation between Daisy, Tom, and Gatsby. In the hotel suite they hear music below, but no one gets up to dance. Daisy attributes this to them getting old, but it is worth considering from that moment on, there is no more dancing, nor any music in the novel.

6. Character analysis - Jay Gatsby

Our uncertainty of Gatsby is mirrored by his own self perception: he is both duplicitous and honest, privileged and disadvantaged, self absorbed and outward looking. From the beginning, the seed of uncertainty is sewn by Nick, when he ascertains that Gatsby 'turned out all right in the end'. This faint praise is the first impression we are given of Jay Gatsby, leading the reader to initially presume much of Gatsby's character is indeed not 'all right'.

Gatsby is a tragic hero, rising and falling in success as he attempts to win the heart of a woman who was undeserving of his love. There is an Aristotelean notion of a 'fatal flaw' or hamartia- a personality trait that causes our tragic hero to be imperfect, and in some way responsible for his own demise. Gatsby's inability to tell the truth, and his determination to recreate the past leads to Daisy's rejection in the hotel suite, and their subsequent journey home 'toward death through the cooling twilight'. In Greek and Shakespearian tragedies, their heroes have noble births: they are kings, princes (sometimes unknowingly so), sons and daughters of houses 'both alike in dignity', and so on. Gatsby has no such connection. However, Fitzgerald does give him a kind of nobility in his rebirth before boarding Dan Cody's boat. This new Gatsby gives himself a different heritage- one where his parents were 'wealthy people in the Middle West' whose 'ancestors have all been educated [at Oxford] for many years.' This artificial history grants Gatsby a noble heritage, and fulfils the traditional expectations of a Greek Tragedy. Fitzgerald appears to be commenting on the American ability to re-invent, and start again, through his presentation of Gatsby as a born again aristocrat. The Mayflower landed on American shores in 1620, and reinvented Europe; some three hundred years later, and Gatsby is on the shore of Lake Superior and is doing the same.

Nick's changeable opinion of Gatsby varies according to what side of Gatsby is being exposed to him. Gatsby the soldier, a fellow veteran, is someone who Carraway feels an immediate affinity for- and during that first party it is the only conversation he has all evening that he seems to enjoy, and feel a connection of 'eternal reassurance' with another human. However, Gatsby falls from Carraway's favour in the time between their first meeting, and the confession of Gatsby's intentions for Daisy. On the morning Gatsby picks him up for his lunch in the city, Nick muses that Gatsby had 'little to say', and is probably a 'person of some undefined consequence'. This Gatsby appears to Carraway to be shallower, and Nick is distrustful of the different stories surrounding his mysterious neighbour, venturing to even speculate that perhaps he was a 'little sinister'. Gatsby rises and falls in Nick's estimations- Nick refers to the point where he believed 'everything and nothing about him' as a 'time of confusion'. Gatsby inspires 'renewals of great faith' in Nick, and through this language Fitzgerald is intimating that their relationship is similar to that of God and worshipper. Fitzgerald depicts Gatsby as a God throughout the novel, Gatsby was the 'son of God' and going 'about His Father's business'. Similarly, Fitzgerald encourages us to echo Nick's opinions of Gatsby: when he doubts, so do we; when he believes, our faith is similarly renewed. In his creation of this flawed and unreliable God, Fitzgerald criticises a society where material possessions are sold as the solution for inner happiness, and where people worship a 'vast, vulgar, and meretricious beauty' over more spiritually enriching pursuits.

Gatsby was the party thrower, but not a party goer- insomuch as he never drinks, never dances, never revels with his revelers. Carraway's first comment that Gatsby was 'all right in the end' seems all the more strange when the reader finishes the novel, and realise that the 'end' Carraway is referring to is Gatsby's death. Nick who admired Gatsby, and assisted Gatsby, and grieves for Gatsby, sees in his friend's death a lesson in modern morality: Gatsby dies so that others can live. This Christ-like sacrifice was unintentional, but Fitzgerald constructs the death so that when Gatsby dies in it provides George a sense of peace- he believes he has avenged his wife's death, before he himself commits suicide. Gatsby's death also excuses Daisy from having to tell him she isn't going to leave her husband after all. And finally, for himself, in dying, Gatsby avoids the suffering he would have had to have endured had he lived and realised that the woman who was his sole desire, was in fact undeserving of his love. The 'careless people' of Tom and Daisy had been careless with Gatsby; he had dreamed too big, and his fall was inevitable. Fitzgerald lambasts the hypocrisy of the post war upper classes, and their focus on 'respectability' over quality of character; Daisy and Tom symbolise the snobbery that had simultaneously enchanted and rejected a young Fitzgerald- desperate to be accepted. Gatsby is never visited in his death- Daisy, who had previously been visiting 'quite often- in the afternoons', stays away, and does not even attend his funeral. Gatsby never has the witness this rejection, and is consequently spared the pain. By the end of the novel, Fitzgerald derides the unreliability of love that comes with caveats. Daisy's love was conditional, and therefore less pure, and never destined to be lasting.

Gatsby did not 'drift coolly out of nowhere and buy a place on Long Island Sound' but instead built his business empire up over five years with the one purpose of enticing Daisy Fay, now Daisy Buchanan, away from her husband and back into his arms. After a lot of back and forth between Gatsby, Jordan, and Nick, his plan finally comes to fruition. The day Gatsby finally is given his opportunity with Daisy, he is a mass of nerves, looking about with 'vacant eyes' and speaking in an 'uncertain voice' as Nick and he wait for Daisy's arrival. In anticipation of her visit, Gatsby has peacocked himself for her- dressing Nick's house with a 'greenhouse' of flowers, and has gilded himself in a 'silver shirt and gold-coloured tie'. Fitzgerald caricatures Gatsby here as a nervous schoolboy, rendered infantile by his love for Daisy. This comically pathetic portrait contrasts sharply with the Gatsby gossiped about at his own parties, where people shared stories about him having 'killed a man'. Here, he is so painfully embarrassed by the situation that he stands at the mantelpiece, a contorted figure of agony, his head 'rested against the clock' in an attempt to lean back and look at ease, so much so that the clock is knocked off and he catches it in his 'trembling hands'. This vignette serves two purposes: one, humorous slapstick, where incredible tension is dispersed by the ridiculousness of Gatsby's hyperbolic response to Daisy's presence; two, a nicely symbolic gesture of Gatsby trying to play with time- the whole meeting with Daisy is intended to allow Gatsby to go back in time, but is unsuccessful- much like his encounter with the clock. It requires Nick, our unexpected hero, to save the day, reprimanding Gatsby with the words 'You're acting like a little boy'. This observation is painful in its honesty; Gatsby's courtship with Daisy is by his account the only courtship he has engaged in during the last five years- and that courtship has mainly taken place metaphysically. Just as much as Gatsby wishes to turn back time, it seems as if he is stuck five years back in his emotional state, and although Daisy is not that naive pre debutant teenager from Louisville, Gatsby is still that young man awed by Daisy and what she represents. Nick leaves the pair, and in his absence they reconnect, and when he returns, the sun is shining and Gatsby 'glowed' and a 'new well being radiated from him'. He smiles 'like an ecstatic patron of recurrent light' at Nick, and the three make their way to Gatsby's house. Fitzgerald cuts through the previous humour with real celebration of the union, and he does so with beautiful prose and light imagery that honours the love of Gatsby and Daisy. It is worth noting that at this point, Daisy has not yet seen Gatsby's house, and she is full of 'unexpected joy' and her voice 'full of aching, grieving beauty'. This is Fitzgerald's hint that on some level, the love between Gatsby and Daisy was sincere and true.

The plan comes together, and Daisy is awed by Gatsby's possessions. As they walk through the gardens, Daisy comments on Gatsby's 'huge' home, and wonders that he lives there 'all alone'. For Daisy, she is filled with admiration, but for Nick, he supposes that there are guests 'concealed behind every couch' so strange it feels to be in Gatsby's house, and it not be crammed full of party goers. On their journey through each room of the house, each is 'swathed in rose and lavender silk', and Nick notes that Gatsby has 'revalued everything in his house according to the measure of response it drew from her well-loved eyes'. Daisy is Gatsby's centre point: everything is measured in relation to her, and his whole world has been orchestrated around her existence, without her even knowing. This highly romantic, and sentimental idea is not expressed sinisterly by Fitzgerald, instead, by depicting Gatsby as a lovestruck fool around Daisy, one who 'nearly toppled down a flight of stairs' in her presence, this obsession is sweet, and innocent. In comparison to Tom, Gatsby is so outward looking, he forgets to take care of himself, whereas Tom is so inward looking, he is shocked when faced with the idea that Daisy has a world that exists 'outside of his own'.

In contrast to Nick's wavering 'faith' in Gatsby, Daisy is a more steady devotee. Although in the time before the events in the novel begin, we are aware of Daisy's faltering faith in Gatsby when Nick supposes she was 'feeling the pressure of the world outside' and in her letters there was a 'nervous despair' which worried Gatsby. Daisy's belief in Gatsby faltered at the beginning, and she married Tom, and then faltered at the end, and she stayed with Tom. Gatsby's behaviour following the crash is that which is almost pitifully depicted: a silent man in the garden of his lover's house, whilst she sat inside 'conspiring' with her husband. Nick leaves for fear of spoiling the 'sacredness of the vigil', implying a solemnity to Gatsby's actions, ironised by the reader's knowledge that Gatsby's belief that the pair are in separate rooms is incorrect, and that they are instead sitting talking over fried chicken. Fitzgerald's contrasting images of gullible trusting Gatsby, and the more cynical self serving Buchanans, further confirms to the reader that Gatsby may have come from lowly beginnings, but his morals are no better than those that were born into more respectable families. Gatsby's crime is important: he is in a car that hits a woman who ran into the road, and doesn't stop. His motivator is Daisy, for whom he will 'of course' take the blame. Tom doesn't stop for two reasons: to avoid being connected to the crime via his wife, and to avoid his connection to Myrtle being revealed. Although both are deplorable, Gatsby manages to be slightly less so. And his misplaced faith in Daisy makes his act of sacrifice all the more pathetic, given that we later find she leaves the state to avoid prosecution, whilst Gatsby stays, and is then slain on the back of Tom's lies. Daisy's most emotionally charged conversation with Gatsby is possibly the shirts conversation. Gatsby, in showing Daisy just how worthy he now is of her, shows her his 'shirts of sheer linen and thick silk and fine flannel' provoking an emotional reaction from Daisy, who 'began to cry stormily' that 'They're such beautiful shirts'. Daisy values Gatsby here in the material goods he has been able to possess, just as Daisy's value rose in Gatsby's eyes due to the other men that had loved her, in return his value increases for equally vacuous reasons. This commercialisation of romantic love mirrors the increasing commercialisation of every aspect of American life in the 1920s. The rise of advertisements in magazines, radio, billboards, newspapers meant that commerce was permeating normal life. This parallel of Daisy's opinion of Gatsby is Fitzgerald's observation of the inevitable commercialisation of the human heart. If Gatsby excites Daisy through the contents of his wardrobe, rather than his physical body or mind, then Gatsby's possessions and financial powers are what Daisy finds attractive. Daisy's influence upon

21

Gatsby is particularly highlighted when the parties stop following her unsuccessful attendance in Chapter Six. Gatsby feels Daisy 'didn't like it' and Nick considers that much of the party 'offends' Daisy. On the doorstep of Nick's home, she and Gatsby share a pleasant half-hour, in the quietness of Nick's home and out of sight of the party. Compared the last moments of the party where they wait on Gatsby's doorstep, waiting for their car. Here, Nick has to listen whilst Daisy and Tom argue over whether the people were 'interesting', with Daisy defending Gatsby, and the origins of his fortune. These two encounters are interesting to compare due to their character traits that they highlight: Gatsby and Daisy's desire for privacy (echoing Jordan's sentiment earlier on in Chapter Three that 'large parties [are] so intimate'), and Daisy and Tom's incompatibility- yet again Fitzgerald gives an insight into the discord in their relationship. Interestingly, Daisy's reaction is to sing, and in doing so exhibits a type of cognitive dissonance (where you exist with two different conflicting emotions) between her state of mind, and her ability to stay with Tom. Daisy both loves Gatsby, and loved Tom- and rather than address the necessary reality to remedy her depression and actually leave Tom, she sings. As Daisy sings, Nick, our reliable observer, watches and imagines Gatsby above, and supposes if a 'radiant young girl' might catch Gatsby's eye and 'blot out' his devotion to Daisy. Daisy is trapped by her marriage and the societal expectations that accompany that, whereas Gatsby is free to other 'romantic possibilities'. Interestingly, this could also be interpreted as Fitzgerald's continuing presentation of Gatsby as a tragic hero- Daisy is the Siren, serenading him below, her voice enchanting him and so therefore he is unwittingly mesmerised and controlled by her, in ways beyond both his comprehension and control. The idea that Gatsby is ploughing ahead totally unable to stop the tragedy that awaits him confirms the idea of Gatsby as a tragic hero, a person who cannot avoid his destiny.

Gatsby's credibility is damaged by his lies. Jordan supposes that Gatsby's Oxford claim was untrue as early as Chapter Three, when she tells Nick 'I don't believe him'. It is via this lie that Tom is able to wedge a gap between Daisy and Gatsby, when his lies regarding his acquisition of his wealth are exposed in the hotel suite in Chapter Seven. Tom declares that 'I found out what your 'drug stores' were', and follows with a string of accusations regarding Gatsby's illegal business endeavours. Up until this point, Daisy has literally and metaphorically stood by him, albeit with a 'visible effort'. However, once this is exposed, Daisy falters, and 'whatever courage she had...was definitely gone.' Gatsby's duplicity is his fatal flaw, and his undoing occurred the moment Tom was able to cast doubt over his past actions. Fitzgerald challenges a society where a person like Gatsby is judged on his past, where people like Daisy and Tom are able to hide their own past indiscretions (the car accident and the affairs) with their affluence. The air of suspicion that clouds people's opinion of Gatsby is created through his own reluctance to admit to his lowly beginnings. Fitzgerald would be acutely aware of high society's snobbery regarding humble beginnings, such as Gatsby's, given his own experiences as a young man attempting to infiltrate higher social circles. Yet, as a modern reader, we perceive Gatsby's success more remarkable given his background. Even when the more unsavoury business activity is taken into account, it is clear that Gatsby is a talented businessman. Gatsby's drive to succeed is an admirable quality, and Fitzgerald romanticises the years of Gatsby as a focused youth in Chapter Nine when Gatsby's father appears. A younger, more innocent Gatsby is depicted- one who was self organised, and self sacrificing, who his father faithfully believed was 'bound to get ahead'. When we contrast this purity to the— unsavoury Tom Buchanan, who has had every opportunity Gatsby didn't have, and yet still chose to dabble in dubious business activities to make his money, Gatsby's mistreatment becomes all the more unjust.

7. Character analysis - Daisy

Daisy is not as simple as her name might lead you to think, Daisy is actually very complicated. Flower imagery follows Daisy everywhere, and the choice of Daisy is interesting as a name. A Daisy (days-eye) is a common flower, typically synonymous with purity and happiness, and this imagery is compounded by Daisy's repeated appearances in white dresses. And yet, despite this whiteness, and purity symbolism, Daisy can seem to be a loathsome, and cowardly character.

If Daisy is loathsome, it is because she has been subjected to loathsome behaviour. It would be too simplistic to dismiss her as a mere society girl. Fitzgerald is careful to detail the fraught relationship between her and Tom: the last minute doubts before the wedding, the car crash with a chambermaid, the sad proclamation at the birth of her daughter- a mirroring of Zelda Fitzgerald's own words. Daisy makes a series of mistakes in the novel, but the worst of all of them has to be the killing of Myrtle. Her cowardice is ultimately the reason for Gatsby's death.

When Nick first visits Daisy and Tom, he and Daisy have an awkward exchange where she tells him she has 'been everywhere and seen everything and done everything' and Nick sees her as asserting herself as a member in a 'rather distinguished little society to which she and Tom belonged.' This foreshadows their later reunion in Chapter Eight when Nick observes them sitting with an 'unmistakable natural intimacy' between them. This inability to leave Tom reveals in Daisy a vulnerability, and Fitzgerald exposes the fickleness of love that within hours of declaring her love for Gatsby, Daisy has returned to Tom, and her old life, and the comforts she finds there.

Daisy is the sole focus for Gatsby- and the person who he has dedicated his life to pursue. Yet, it feels as if the idea of Daisy, rather than the actual Daisy, is the object of Gatsby's desires. In Chapter Eight, Gatsby confides in Nick, and tells him the story of his and Daisy's love affair. Daisy is described as a commodity who Gatsby felt had 'increased in value' due to the number of men who were already in love with her. This dehumanisation elevates, rather than degenerates her, to Gatsby, who views her as an almost ethereal being. When Tom previously supposed that Gatsby would have only met Daisy if he 'brought the groceries to the back door.' that belief is shared, to an extent, to Gatsby's wonder that he ever found his way to Daisy's house, calling it a 'colossal accident' and aware that it was only his 'invisible cloak' that permitted him access. In the time that passes, Daisy becomes a different person, and Gatsby struggles with this adjustment. Not only does he stare at Daisy's daughter 'with surprise' and Nick considers that Gatsby hadn't 'really believed in its existence before'. Gatsby also expresses his frustration to Nick that Daisy 'doesn't understand…she used to be able to understand' and that Gatsby wished for Daisy to 'obliterate' the past by rejecting Tom, and agreeing to marry Gatsby. Fitzgerald acknowledges the implausibility of this cause through the voice of Nick: 'You can't repeat the past'. But it falls on deaf ears. The brief affair that Daisy and Gatsby conducted took place in a different world: America was so fundamentally altered by the war that when peacetime arrived, then there came with it a feeling of seismic change. This epochal shift leaves Gatsby pining for a woman who would never be in his grasp; in this new world, the old world rules of courtship and society still remain. In breaking off their engagement and marrying Tom, it could be seen that Daisy made an error in judgement, but marrying the wrong person is a common enough mistake, and Daisy would be the one to pay the most dearly for it.

However, when Daisy fails Gatsby at the moment she admits she did love Tom once, that is the moment the reader sympathises with Daisy the most. Daisy gives herself away in her own home, sat around the dinner table where she had dined with her family, in the most domestic of situations, with the words: 'You always look so cool'. In that moment, Daisy has let her mask slip, and her husband sees her for what she is- in love with another man. The hypocrisy of his anger is later lambasted when Nick notes the parallels in Tom and George at the gas station, but for now, Tom's incandescent anger is directed at Gatsby, and Daisy, who has been faithful to Tom up until this point, would be pitied by the reader, given it was around this very table just a few months earlier, Daisy had to listen whilst Tom argued on the phone with his mistress. By revealing the affaire in this way, Fitzgerald is building the sympathy for Daisy, so when in the hotel suite she is unable to fulfil Gatsby's fantasy of 'obliterating' the past. Daisy attempts to appease him, saying with 'perceptible reluctance' that she never loved Tom, and when Tom provokes her in his 'husky' voice, Daisy protests 'please don't.' Daisy reneges at that point, and pleads with Gatsby that he wants 'too much'. Although Gatsby has been living his life for Daisy, Daisy was living her life for herself, and in this way it would be impossible for the real Daisy to live up to the fantasy idea of Daisy that Gatsby had been chasing- the pedestal was too high, and memories too unreliable. Daisy was not the girl she was back when Gatsby first met her. She had been cuckolded, she had become a mother, she had become disillusioned. When Gatsby mourns that she no longer 'understands', that understanding is not clarified, but Fitzgerald here appears to be challenging out understanding of Gatsby's love- and that in a way it comes with as many conditions as Daisy's. Daisy required wealth, but Gatsby required perfection.

Daisy's only confidante appears to be Jordan, a woman who openly gossips about Tom's affair with Nick within only minutes of meeting him. Jordan is unworried by the morality of assisting Gatsby with his intention of romancing Daisy, and plays her own part in the beginning of their affair. The reader is never privy to any private conversation between Jordan and Daisy, the structural restriction of first person narration would make that quite problematic, and yet, there is never any suggestion that the two confide any deep feelings with one and other. We know from the teasing about kisses the day of the crash that the two must speak about their respective relationships, Daisy rebukes Jordan's protests with a playful 'You kiss Nick too' revealing not just the closeness of their relationship, but simultaneously hinting at the depth to which Nick conceals parts of the story, further confirming for the reader of his unreliability as a narrator.

Daisy and Dan Cody's partner, Ella Kaye, are an interesting pair to contrast and compare. Nick observes that Ella Kaye was Dan Cody's 'Madame de Maintenton', and within a week of her arrival on the yacht, Dan Cody died. The allusion to the French King Louis XIV's unofficial wife reveals a lot about the character of Ella Kaye. Madame de Maintenon was a woman of a lower class who was unable to be officially recognised as the King's wife, but influenced him sufficiently to stop the King from taking a mistress, and take her advice regarding laws and decisions on running the country. Ella Kaye and Daisy Buchanan are both women who are in relationships with men who are of a different class to them, who have a significant amount of money, who influence their decisions (Daisy to close down the parties, Ella Kaye Cody's extended holiday) and whose partners die quickly after their reappearance following an absence. By paralleling the two women in this way, Fitzgerald can be seen as using women as a symbol for the fallibility of men. The part that Daisy plays in Gatsby's downfall is a manifestation of Gatsby's hubris- he falls because of his weakness for Daisy, just as other men before him have fallen.

8. Character analysis - Nick

Nick Carraway is our flawed and unreliable narrator. Throughout the novel, we question the reliability of his account, from the initial posthumous warning of Nick's father that if Nick should 'feel like criticising any one' then Nick should 'remember that all the people in this world haven't had the advantages' Nick has had. On the surface this could be interpreted as merely useful fatherly advice, yet by the end of the novel, we see that Mr Carraway Snr probably had just cause for giving such a warning. Nick insists that he is 'one of the few honest people that I have ever known' following the revelation that not only is he attached to someone through a 'vague understanding' back home in the East, but that he now intends to break it off to leave him free to pursue Jordan. The flawed part of Nick's character kicks in here- as he is seemingly oblivious that his criticism of Jordan's 'dishonesty' seems rather weak, given he himself is romantically and has concealed it, from not only us the readers, but also to his friends and family, when he was asked outright by Tom in Chapter One, and Nick refutes it, claiming 'libel' despite admitting he was signing weekly letters 'Love, Nick' by the end of Chapter Two. He sees himself as an outsider, the observer of dreadful behaviour, and above the immorality of his friends and family. Nick, who colludes in the infidelity of his cousin's husband, who stays at Gatsby's parties until the other guests have left and gone to bed, who leaves one woman back West to go East, and then leaves a different woman East to go West. When Nick tells Gatsby he is better than the others at the end of the novel, it would be fair to include himself in that. Nick's inability to recognise his own flaws is something that is shared with the rest of humanity. Fitzgerald presents Nick as earnest, and keen to be doing the right thing, and yet failing miserably. Perhaps it is this that makes 'The Great Gatsby' such an enduring text, as along with Nick, we the reader are blind to our flaws, and justifying the dreadful things we do to the ones closest to us, all the while pointing out the flaws in others. The Biblical expression of 'removing the bark from your eye before pointing out the splinter in someone else's' is called to mind. Fitzgerald both mocks and condones Nick, and in this way we can see him as a storyteller most like ourselves.

Nick's proximity to the action allows him an insight into the lives of others, despite his comparatively lower status. When Nick first wanders into Gatsby's party he has a miserable time, with the exception of the conversation with the (at the time) anonymous Gatsby. Surrounded by glittering opulence, Nick enjoys a brief conversation about the grey days of wartime in France. In between the discussion in the library over the 'real' books, and then gossiping about their host's source of income, Nick meets Gatsby and they share their memories of 'wet, gray little villages' from their time in the war. These muted colours contrast to the 'yellow dresses' and 'silver scales' that have been described just paragraphs before. By structuring the conversation in this way, Fitzgerald deifies their wartime memories, by characterising them as something 'real' in contrast to the pomp and grandeur of the party, and the life that Gatsby has now carved out for himself. Fitzgerald gives Nick a little bit of credibility at this point, when the posturing and ego are stripped away, we have two men that bond over their shared experience. This is not a tale of male friendship, but at this point, Fitzgerald recognises a human desire to connect over shared experiences, and the 'eternal reassurance' Nick finds in Gatsby's smile highlights to the audience not just Gatsby's charisma, but also Nick's evident loneliness in the West, and foreshadows his eventual return home.

If you chart the friendship between Nick and Gatsby, you would see that the dips and peaks track where Nick perceives Gatsby to be more or less truthful. Nick craves honesty as much as he shies away from it. Nick avoids honesty regarding his romantic connections continually throughout the novel- beginning with his denial that he was involved by claiming he was 'too poor' giving deliberately obtuse replies to the inquiries as to whether he was engaged despite admitting to the reader that 'of course I knew what they were referring to'. Nick makes little progressive here, and repeats the pattern of running away from a location when the story opens he has come east because 'gossip had published the banns', the story ends with his return, but this time he meets with Jordan to officially break it off before he moves. Jordan and he share a rather brutal but honest conversation in chapter nine, right at the very end of the novel, where Jordan calls out Nick on his self belief that he is an 'honest, straightforward person', and here we see Nick finally exhibit some inner growth when he concedes that he is 'too old to lie to himself and call it honour.' Nick's concession marks a change in his self perception, and in doing so Fitzgerald elevates Nick in our estimations. He is no longer the self deluded saviour of truth, but instead a man who is still 'half in love' with a woman he has betrayed, and finally able to admit his own imperfections.

With regards to Gatsby, Nick desires to know the truth behind the Oxford claims, and the origins of his wealth, and along with all the other characters, Nick himself speculates the origins of his fortune. However, unlike the others, Gatsby chooses Nick to confide in, and reveals to Nick the some of the truth regarding how he came into money. Gatsby's own dishonesty towards Nick can be interpreted as indicative to Gatsby's own feelings towards Nick. These inconsistencies, where he tells Nick in Chapter Four that he was 'educated at Oxford' and Nick notes that he 'swallowed' the words, suspecting him of deception- but then later is shown a photograph, and Nick oscillates back to believing it 'all true'. When Gatsby finally reveals the complete truth of his Oxford education in Chapter Seven, Nick experiences a 'complete renewal in faith' that he had 'experienced before'. The reference to Nick's 'renewal in faith' implies something almost religious about Nick and Gatsby's relationship. Gatsby is described using both Christian and Greek allusions, when Nick claims Gatsby was a 'Platonic conception', and the 'son of God', we see Gatsby as deity, and Nick the doubting Thomas (a follower of Jesus who only believed he had risen again when he was able to place his hands in his wounds). The follower/leader dynamic becomes problematic when we see Gatsby as could be seen to be just as inconsistent, or at least, self serving. Gatsby uses Nick to get close to Daisy, and then once the reunion has taken place, every conversation the two of them have centres around Daisy, and Gatsby's desire to recreate the past. Even Gatsby's original conversation with Nick becomes discoloured for the reader when we are given the information that Gatsby has sought Nick out as a gateway to his main goal: obtaining Daisy. Jordan discloses to Nick that Gatsby needs Nick to arrange the meeting because Gatsby 'wants [Daisy] to see his house' and Nick's house is 'right next door'. This geographical, rather than emotional motivator for their friendship exposes Gatsby as a more Machiavellian character, be it one who is so crippled by his romantic notions that he 'read a Chicago paper for years just on the chance of catching a glimpse' of his ex lover's name. Whether Nick resents Gatsby for this, we do not know, Nick never comments on it directly. However, he continues to collude with Gatsby, and permits him to use his home as a meeting point for their affair, not just once, but again when Gatsby hosts both Tom and Daisy at his home for a party. After a 'conservative foxtrot' when Nick sees Gatsby dance for the first time, Gatsby and Daisy steal away to spend a cordial half an hour on the steps of Nick's house- with Nick chaperoning 'In case there's a fire, or a flood'. Nick observes that 'except for the half-hour she's been alone with Gatsby she wasn't having a good time'. Nick seems to wish to assist Gatsby in any way he can, serving him to deliver Daisy to Gatsby as a kind of offering to please him. And yet, despite Nick's assistance, and Daisy's willingness to reunite, Gatsby is not happy. Nick is aware of his unhappiness, and trivialises his distress by remonstrating Gatsby after Gatsby complains of Daisy's lack of 'understanding' that Gatsby shouldn't 'ask too much of her.'. Nick's realism jars against Gatsby's romantic sentimentality, and Fitzgerald presents these two men as opposing sides of the reality versus fantasy approach to love. Gatsby views Daisy as flawless, and is overcome with a desire to 'return to a certain starting place' then Gatsby would be able to recapture his perfect love; Nick views Jordan in far more caustic terms- she is 'incurably dishonest', and Nick blames himself for 'slow-thinking' for the glacial speed in which their relationship moves. In Chapter Four when Nick describes what we can assume is their first act of intimacy, Jordan's mouth is 'wan, scornful', and she moves 'jauntily'. Neither man ends up with the object of their affection, and Fitzgerald seems to condemn both approaches. Daisy and Tom are the only ones who remain together, and yet Fitzgerald doesn't glorify their union either. In this world there are no happy unions, and no simple romances. The corruption of the modern world renders them unable to partake in relationships where you would be required to remain faithful, vulnerable, and honest.

9. Character analysis- Jordan Baker

Jordan's profession simultaneously sets her apart from the rest of the characters, whilst also providing her with a commonality to the rest. Jordan is a professional golfer, something that Nick doesn't realise until after they had spent the day together, when he recognises her 'pleasing contemptuous expression' from sports magazines. Of all the characters, Jordan is the only one who is genuinely famous, and famous for the merits of her talents. However, it is through the golf we know that Jordan is a duplicitous character, as she 'moved her [golf] ball…in a semi-final', a story that never 'reached the newspapers', but that Nick has heard anyway.

Fitzgerald uses the friendship of Jordan and Daisy to provide an insight into the life of Daisy. It is through Jordan we learn in Chapter Four of Tom's behaviour with 'one of the chambermaids from the Santa Barbara Hotel' shortly after they return from their honeymoon. This is something that Daisy hints at in the hotel suite when she tells Tom she never loved him in Chapter Seven. Tom's other misdemeanours are outlined to Nick: Jordan also serves to deliver Daisy to Gatsby, and just like Nick, she shows no loyalty to Tom. In acting as the go between, Jordan seems to stir in Nick an amorous emotion, and Nick begins to hear the phrase 'There are only the pursued, the pursuing, the busy and the tired' beat in his mind. Fitzgerald offers Jordan and Nick's relationship as an echo of Daisy and Gatsby. Just as Gatsby is 'look[ing]…wildly…in the shadow' for the past 'just out of reach', their story provides Jordan and Nick for their own inspiration for their own relationship, that they conduct in the shadows of their friends. Fitzgerald could be interpreted as presenting their love as ill-fated as the couple who inspired it, and when Nick returns East he fulfils his inevitable destiny, and completes the circular narrative of a man fleeing a relationship to avoid commitment.

Jordan and Nick meet accidentally at Gatsby's party, following their more orchestrated encounter at the Buchanan home. At the point where Nick was becoming 'roaring drunk' out of 'sheer embarrassment' from being on his own, he spies Jordan, and immediately attaches himself to her, feeling it 'necessary' in order to allow him to make 'cordial remarks' to the other party goers. Here, Jordan acts as a crutch to Nick's social anxieties. It is only in her company that he feels he can speak to the other guests and socialise. Jordan has come with an 'escort' who was a 'persistent undergraduate given to violent innuendo', but Nick steals her away from him, and they spend much of the night together. Fitzgerald presents their meeting as one that services Nick, rather than Jordan. Nick takes Jordan's 'slender golden arm' and together they navigate the party. Through Jordan's presence, Nick feels at ease. Nick's feelings towards Jordan are somewhat ambivalent- his description of her 'jauntiness' and admittance that he enjoyed attending social occasions because 'everyone knew her name' hints at Nick's shallow pursuit of friendships that are based upon social standing, rather than quality of character. Nick felt he 'wasn't actually in love' rather a 'tender curiosity'. The first person narration lends the reader to feel more supportive towards Nick's feelings, however, Fitzgerald's sympathetic depiction of Jordan does cause the reader to question how Nick's mistreatment of Jordan reveals an unpleasant side to his character.

Nick ascertains that Jordan 'avoided clever, shrewd men' and that Jordan 'felt safer on a plane where any divergence from a code would be thought impossible'. Nick is implying that Jordan requires gullibility in order to manipulate those around her into believing her lies. Jordan claims she prefers large parties for their 'intimacy', revealing a predilection for opportunities to speak confidentially, and conduct herself in a way that may not be permitted so openly. The somewhat sexually charged claim that Jordan begun lying young in order to 'satisfy the demands of her hard, jaunty body' repeats that adjective that Nick uses over and over again to describe Jordan. 'Jaunty' implies confidence, rather than sensuality, and perhaps in describing Jordan as such, Fitzgerald is making a comment upon the new kind of woman that the modern world was creating: one that could be athletic, independent, and in control of her own sexuality. Every single description of Jordan contains the word 'jaunty' in some form. In 1908 Havelock Ellis published 'Studies in the Psychology of Sex: Sexual Inversion' where he describes the practices of homosexual females, and describes the behaviour of 'mannish woman'. The American sexual politics of the early 20th Century were concerned with the emergence of homosexual behaviour, and the idea of female sexual pleasure. Conservative American society was rocked by the shock of not just the idea that women could enjoy sex, but that people of the same sex could be engaged in relationships. Fitzgerald could be implying through the description of Jordan's 'jaunty' body that perhaps Jordan Baker was similar to the real life 'Josaphine Baker' (a chorus girl and entertainer, loved by Fitzgerald's friends Hemingway and Picasso) who was famous for her lesbian relationships.

Jordan's loyalty and reliability is inconsistent in the novel. She is apparently loyal to Daisy, and yet is keen to share the information that 'Tom's got a woman in New York', and openly eavesdrops on the argument Daisy and Tom have when Myrtle's phone calls disrupt their meal during Nick's first visit in Chapter One. Just as Jordan was keen to gossip about Tom and his mistress, she participates in the gossip about Gatsby with similar vigour. When the two girls in the yellow dresses share their own inside information on Gatsby, the women 'leaned in together confidentially' and Nick notes that a 'thrill passed over all of us' at the news that Gatsby supposedly 'killed a man'. Fitzgerald creates a character who is seemingly drawn towards gossip, and delights in the scandal of others, whilst she herself was known for her own brush with an incident that 'approached the proportions of a scandal' when she was caught up in a claim she had cheated in a golfing tournament. Jordan's loyalty to Nick is also perceived to be unreliable- in Chapter Four, when Gatsby takes Nick out for lunch in the city, Nick jumps to the incorrect conclusion that Gatsby is interested in Jordan, asking him 'Do you mean you're in love with Miss Baker?'. Nick's assumption that there is a relationship forming between a woman he is involved with and his friend, indicates that Nick does not fully trust Jordan, and has little expectation of her fidelity. Additionally, through his question, Nick could be interpreted as giving away the extent to his feelings of attachment to Miss Baker, who he has only previously described as someone who 'for a moment' he 'thought' he loved.

Jordan and Nick's relationship dies the same night as Myrtle's body is destroyed by Gatsby's car. Earlier in the day, all seems as normal between them, and there is references to the intimacy between them when Daisy reminds a teasing Jordan that 'you kiss Nick too'. Even after the revelation of Gatsby and Daisy's affair, Nick places Jordan as on his side, when Tom is ranting 'incessantly', Nick considers him 'as remote from Jordan and me' as the noise on the sidewalk. By positioning himself with Jordan, we can see Nick considering a future with Jordan. On the realisation it is his birthday, Nick acknowledges that with thirty it brings a 'thinning list of single men to know' and consoles himself with the thought that he has 'Jordan beside me, who, unlike Daisy, was too wise ever to carry well-forgotten dreams for age to age'. This praising thought it possible the kindest description Nick ever bestows upon Jordan. Here, Fitzgerald is leading the reader to believe that Nick and Jordan will end up together, and that Nick finds in Jordan a more genuine kind of realistic love, than the love we have just seen torn apart between Gatsby and Daisy. And yet, by the end of the night, on the doorstep of the Buchanan home, Nick finds himself reluctant to go in, and considers that he had 'had enough of them...that included Jordan too' and decides he 'wanted to be alone' feeling 'sick' after what had happened with Myrtle. Nick's disgust appears to stem from the lack of accountability any of them take in the death of Myrtle. At the crime scene, no one gives Gatsby or Daisy's name, and they collude in Tom's cover-up of Daisy's involvement with her death, knowing that if he were to tell the police it was Gatsby's car, then his own connection to Myrtle would be inevitably revealed. Nick plays his own part in this, telling the policeman that they have 'come straight from New York', to distance themselves from the crime, and Tom 'whispered' to Nick 'Let's get out' and Nick acquiesces without protest. And yet, when they return to the house, Fitzgerald implies that Nick's own feelings of guilt are now overwhelming him, and he is 'feeling a little sick' and 'a little weird'.

The next morning, Nick calls Jordan and during their tense conversation Jordan tells Nick that she has 'left Daisy's house' and this 'annoyed' Nick despite him admitting that 'it had been tactful' for her to do so. This double standard symbolises the impossibility that faces Jordan at this point: she has done nothing wrong, but can do nothing right. Nick's unreliability as a narrator rears its head again here, when he claims that he doesn't 'know which of us hung up', and yet later, Jordan reveals that it was during that very conversation that Nick 'threw [her] over'. Fitzgerald exposes the contrasting experience of males and females in their relationships through this contrasting interpretation of the same event. Jordan perceives this phone call to have ended their relationship, whereas Nick felt that it still required ending. Jordan tells Nick that she is 'engaged to another man' but Nick 'doubted that'. This distrust echoes all the previous examples of Nick's assertions that Jordan was dishonest, but also the very fact that she says it displays a vulnerability in Jordan, indicative that her feelings towards Nick were sincere, and her confusion over his motivations for ending their relationship have troubled her. Jordan tells Nick that although she doesn't 'give a damn about you now' the period following the ending of their relationship was 'a new experience…I felt dizzy for a while'. Jordan lashes out at Nick, telling him she thought herself 'careless' for believing him an 'honest, straightforward' person. Jordan is the only character in the entire novel to challenge Nick on his assertion that he is honest, and in doing so, acts as the voice of the reader, who at this point would feel similarly towards Nick. Fitzgerald evokes tenderness for the pair of them, when Nick vocally admits his own faults, and inwardly feels 'tremendously sorry'.

10. Character analysis - Tom Buchanan

The easily rich and powerful Tom Buchanans of this world can be found everywhere you may care to look for them. Tom is consistently unpleasant and unlikeable, and it is easy to imagine that Fitzgerald drew upon his own experiences of attending a privileged school and college in his creation of the character.

Before we hear of Tom's wealth, Nick is quick to note his physical appearance and sporting success: a 'powerful end' and a 'national figure' who reached 'limited excellence' in football. Daisy describes him as 'hulking' and it is intriguing that she draws attention to a her 'black and blue' little finger, that Tom has hurt although she says she knows he 'didn't mean to'. This injury foreshadows the later punching of Myrtle in Chapter Two, giving a small taste of Tom's ability to physically harm the women who love him. Nick's description of Tom's body is charged with a mixture of admiration and jealousy- he describes his 'enormous power' in the 'great pack of muscle' of his 'cruel body'. Yet, there is criticism laced into his admiration: 'shining arrogant eyes' and 'supercilious manner' reveal Nick's reservations about his old college friend. Nick finds Tom's overt physicality intimidating, and purports to feel that Tom disregards Nick's opinions because Tom considers himself to be 'stronger and more of a man than you are'. This presentation of masculinity as being reliant upon physical capabilities is something that Fitzgerald struggled with during his own college years when he attempted to succeed in sport; here Fitzgerald could be rebuking the popular belief that manliness is connected to physical strength, by using a character as contemptible as Tom as a physical embodiment of those typical masculine values. Tom uses his physical power to not only control the women around him, but also Nick. When Nick first meets Myrtle, Nick notes that Tom's 'determination to have my company boarded on violence', and 'literally forced' Nick to disembark the train. When Nick sees Tom for the last time at the end of the novel, again he is described as moving in an 'aggressive way' and Nick notes the position of his hands that appear to be ready to 'fight off interference'. Initially, Tom tries to convince Nick that Tom told George Wilson that it was Gatsby driving the car out of fear of him when he came to their house. Wilson, the 'anaemic' looking garage owner makes an unlikely fearsome opponent to a man as powerful as Tom, and when he realises Nick would not buy it, he 'broke off defiantly' and admits he did it because he felt Gatsby 'had it coming'.

The story of Tom and Daisy's wedding is first told by Jordan, in Chapter Four, when Jordan finally reveals Gatsby's intentions towards Daisy, and in doing so details to Nick the happenings that occurred whilst he was away at war. Jordan recounts how following a brief period of apparent chastity, Daisy was 'engaged to a man from New Orleans, In June she married Tom Buchanan of Chicago'. This swift change in favour is typical of Daisy's fickle nature, flitting from one man to another, and yet- there is the suggestion that Gatsby was the man for Daisy, when we presume who was the one she was crying for the night before her wedding when she got 'drunk as a monkey' and putting the expensive string of pearls Tom had bought her in the waste paper basket, telling Jordan to 'tell 'em Daisy's change her mine'. Daisy destroys a letter, we can suppose is from Gatsby, before sobering up and the next day marries Tom 'without so much of a shiver'. The wedding is full of 'pomp and circumstance' its extravagance reaching that of Gatsby's own excess, with a 'whole floor of the Muhbach hotel' hired out to them. Later, we hear of their wedding again when in the hotel suite Jordan and Daisy compare how similar the heat on that day was to the wedding day, and Jordan recounts a wedding guest who fainted and then subsequently wouldn't leave her house until instructed to three weeks later. During the course of the conversation, it is discovered that the wedding guest had found his way into the wedding through fraudulent means, claiming to know Daisy when he didn't. This foreshadows quite neatly, the conversation that follows with regards to Gatsby's own vague past. Fitzgerald's emphasis upon the wedding and the connected events, that consumes two lengthy descriptions at two separate points in the novel could be seen as deriding the increasing popularity of the upper classes to throw extravagant wedding parties. A wedding has both legal and religious functions- but when the God is capitalism and indulgence, then weddings like Daisy and Tom's, with Tom who 'came down with a hundred people in four private cars' and gifts that are worth $350 000 (in today's money, over 4.5 million dollars) appear to be over indulgent, and superfluous, especially given that it took place whilst soldiers like Nick were away fighting in the war.

Tom's infidelity is the crack that fractures his marriage to Daisy. Soon after they are married, we learn that Tom was caught with 'one of the chambermaids' from the 'Santa Barbara Hotel', from Jordan in Chapter Four, and earlier in Chapter One, we already have discovered that at the birth of their daughter that Tom was 'God knows where' leaving Daisy to feel 'utterly abandoned'. Earlier in the same chapter we learn about Myrtle his 'woman in New York' when she telephones during lunch when Nick is visiting. Tom himself confesses in the hotel suite that 'once in a while' he goes 'off on a spree', to which Daisy calls him 'revolting'. The psychological damage this does to Daisy is intimated from the very first chapter when Daisy confesses to Nick that she feels 'pretty cynical about everything' because she has had 'a very bad time'. Her wish that her daughter be a 'beautiful little fool' can be interpreted as a wish for her to be oblivious to the inevitable harm a woman feels when the man she loves mistreats her, as Tom has mistreated Daisy. Tom has damaged Daisy so much, that she cannot envisage a world where her daughter won't be subjected to that kind of mistreatment, and she appears to be spiritually broken by her experience. Yet, she stays with Tom, and even when given the opportunity to leave, she chooses to stay. Nick observes the two of them in Chapter Seven, where they 'weren't happy…and yet they weren't unhappy either'. Instead they had an air of 'natural intimacy' and a look as if they were 'conspiring together'. Nick groups Daisy and Tom together as 'careless people…they smashed things…and retreated back into their money'. Tom's influence over Daisy changes her irreversibly, and she is no longer the woman that Gatsby remembers from their first meeting only five years before. Fitzgerald could be commenting on the toxic impact Tom has had over Daisy, and his power to pollute people who were once good people.

Tom and Myrtle's affair reveal the most unpleasant aspects of Tom's character: the violence, the mistreatment of his mistress' husband, and the extent of his duplicity. In Chapter Two Nick is taken by Tom into the city, and Tom introduces Nick to his mistress, Myrtle. Fitzgerald reaffirms the reader's feelings that Tom is a deeply unpleasant character, with her confidence that Nick will not reveal to Daisy where Tom has taken him, and knows, without even asking, that Nick will collude with the cover up of his affair. Despite Nick's insistence that he is 'honest', Nick never tells Daisy about his day and night with Tom and Myrtle, and instead stands by and watches whilst Tom cuckolds his cousin. At the garage, Tom speaks to George Wilson, 'slapping him jovially' and telling him 'coldly' that the car sale can be called off if George keeps pushing him to sell it. George is 'blond, spiritless…anaemic' and Tom derides his trusting nature telling Nick 'He's so dumb he doesn't know he's alive.' Fitzgerald mirrors the disparity of wealth in society through wealthy Tom's exploitation of poor George. America's wealth is built upon the exploitation of the poor by those with power and money; likewise, Tom is able to behave as he wishes, because of George's poverty and stupidity. At the party at the flat Tom rents for Myrtle, Nick has to endure the awkwardness of Tom and Myrtle's absence, when he returns from buying cigarettes, he realises they have 'disappeared' presumably to the bedroom, and he sits and waits 'discreetly' for them to reappear. This flagrant behaviour is tolerated by our 'honest' narrator, and reveals the depth to which Tom is happy to transgress his marriage vows, regardless to who he is in the house with. Comparing this to Gatsby and Daisy's 'conservative foxtrot' in Chapter Six, makes Tom's behaviour all the more deplorable. Myrtle's romantic and sentimental retelling of her first meeting with Tom on the train has no impact upon Nick, and instead we are given his account of the entire night almost without any personal comment- when Tom and Myrtle quarrel, Nick merely notes 'Tom Buchanan broke her nose with his open hand.' Fitzgerald adopts this detached tone possibly to mimic Nick's discomfort at the socially awkward situation he finds himself in, or perhaps to recreate the detached feeling a person experiences whilst intoxicated, as Nick himself is drunk. Tom's anger at Myrtle saying his wife's name could inspire some interpretation that perhaps Tom does harbour feelings of love towards his wife, and the pain of hearing his mistress say her name brings him the discomfort of having to reconcile his own behaviour with his marriage vows. Alternatively, Tom's anger could have been inspired by his desire to control the entire situation to his own liking- just as he strong-arms Nick out of the train carriage because he wants Nick to meet his mistress, Tom uses his fists to stop Myrtle from doing that which he doesn't want her to do. Myrtle's sister Catherine reveals that Tom has lied to Myrtle regarding the reason why he won't leave Daisy, telling Nick that Daisy is 'a Catholic, and they don't believe in divorce.' Nick is 'a little shocked at the elaborateness of the lie' conveying to the reader the innocence of Nick in this entire situation, and his unease at being caught up in this unsavoury conversation. At the point Tom realises what has been happening between Gatsby and Daisy, he was 'astounded' and he looked at Daisy 'as if he just recognised her as someone he knew a long time ago.' This disconnect between Tom's expectation of Daisy, and the person who Daisy is, evidences Tom's lack of understanding of his own wife. Possibly, Fitzgerald is suggesting at this point Tom has realised the consequences of his own infidelities, or, in the five years that have passed, Tom is reminded of the Daisy who he married, who was loved by many men, and was engaged to marry at least two other men before he married her himself. Tom is incredulous when Daisy drives off towards New York, and he tells Jordan and Nick that he has a 'second sight'. Even when Tom is faced with the shocking news of his wife's affair, he must boast about his own knowledge and capabilities. This arrogance could be the reason for his friends' rather unsympathetic reaction- Jordan asking him questions 'humorously' and the pair 'laughed'. Fitzgerald has created such an unpleasant character in Tom that the lack of sympathy from Jordan and Nick feels well deserved. As a reader, we feel a sense of catharsis at this point, as a feel of satisfaction that Tom has finally received what he has given out to Daisy for years. When George and Tom meet in Chapter Eight, the pair now share the misfortune of both having been made aware of their partner's indiscretions. Nick notes that there was 'no difference between men' at the sight of George, looking as sick as Tom did. Both had been betrayed and made aware that their partners had 'some sort of life apart from' their husbands. Fitzgerald here acknowledges the commonality of all men, that all desire the same things, and are shaken by the same revelations, regardless of background. Tom may have thought Wilson 'too dumb to know he was alive' back in Chapter Two, but now he realised that his pride has come before his fall, and he too has been 'dumb' to Daisy's affair. At the sight of the crash, Tom is initially tantalised by the prospect of the car crash, until he realises that the person who has been hit was Myrtle. As they drive away Tom 'whimpered' and calls Gatsby a 'coward'. Fitzgerald uses the irony of Tom's insult to further establish Tom as an unsympathetic and deluded character; whilst condemning Gatsby or cowardice, he himself drives away from an accident where he knows information that would indicate the killer, because he himself is too cowardly to have his affair exposed. Furthermore, Fitzgerald chooses to deride Tom's character by having him tell Nick that he has had his 'share of suffering' because he 'cried like a baby' when he saw Myrtle's box of dog biscuits on the sideboard.   This paltry example of 'suffering' compared to Gatsby losing his life, consolidates our opinion that Tom is an inward looking egocentric man.

Tom and his love rival Gatsby seemingly share little in their physicality. Although both young, Gatsby is merely described as 'tanned skin drawn attractively across his face'. There is none of Tom's physical impressiveness, and indeed, even as a young man we are only told that Gatsby's body was 'hardening' indicating a process, rather than a finished result. Financially, Tom has come from a family so rich he was able to buy a 'string of polo ponies' as well as the 'string of pearls' and Nick finds it 'hard' that someone of his 'own generation' was able to do that. Fitzgerald contrasts the two lovers in their sentimentality, and their lack of it. The courtship of Gatsby and Daisy is full of romantic descriptions of natural imagery- the moonlight, the foliage, whereas for Tom it is all practical. Daisy has her debut and they are engaged. Tom and Gatsby's clothes are also notable in their difference: Tom's 'swank' of his riding clothes are 'strained' with the muscles beneath, whereas Gatsby's softer fabrics of 'sheer linen and thick silk and fine flannel' portray an impression of a softer, more gentle man.

The attitude that the rise of Black culture in America was in some way damaging to White culture is embodied in Tom Buchanan. As mentioned in the section on The Jazz Age, North America's mass immigration hit a peak the decade before 'The Great Gatsby' was written, in 1910, and subsequently America's culture was altered forever, with a fusion of European, African, and Asian cultures populating the towns and cities. Unsurprisingly, this change was one that was embraced with varying degrees of warmth- with many American's expressing Xenophobic views, fearing that White people would lose their power as their position as the majority race slipped. From Chapter One, Tom is sermonising on the subject of race, and warns Nick that 'Civilisation's going to pieces' and that Nick should 'look out', and yet, no one else takes his words seriously, with Daisy 'winking ferociously' when she agrees with him and Tom 'impatiently' glancing at her when she interrupts his speech. This news in received by Nick disdainfully, and he describes his concentration when speaking on the matter as 'pathetic'. Fitzgerald is here castigating the opinion that nordic races are inherently better, by using Tom as a mouthpiece for the views. Tom is such an unlikeable character, by having him hold these opinions, it intimates to the reader that Fitzgerald feels that these ideas are ridiculous. In Chapter Seven, when the affair between Gatsby and Daisy has been revealed, Tom's rant about Gatsby and his behaviour extends into his disgust for 'intermarriage between black and white'. Nick sees this as 'impassioned gibberish' and Tom's conflation of the two issues indicates a weakness of mind that reaches for racial insults when put under pressure. Tom's hatred for black people stems from his own insecurities: just as he fears he will lose his wife, he fears white men will lose power to black. Thus when presented with a future without Daisy, his response is to return to his racist ramblings, as those fears of emasculation stem from the same place. In this way, Fitzgerald paints a sorry picture of Tom, a figure of the 'old' world, frightened by the changes afoot in the new world.

11. Fitzgerald's use of themes

The American Dream and Money

In its original incarnation, the 'American Dream' is the idea that anybody can succeed if they work hard enough- class will not hold them back. Over time, it has come to mean the obtaining of material possessions that in themselves are signs of wealth and affluence. Money in this novel can be split into old and new- with Gatsby and his 'self made man' narrative firmly in the 'new' camp. In the 1920s social mobility permitted the working classes to acquire money at a rate never before known. This disruption to the social classes was met with mixed reactions: some resented the apparent appearance of respectability in the newcomers; some felt that this was the embodiment of the American dream, and that money, old and new, should be valued the same. Old money was considered more respectable because it was acquired through the nobility of birth- land was inherited; there were expectations regarding the level of education received, and control over marriages commonplace. The old money has a veneer of respectability, with the manners of the 'old world' society dictating etiquette that Gatsby hopelessly fails to grasp. An example of this arises when the Sloanes invite Gatsby to come to their party, with absolute insincerity, Mrs Sloane invites Gatsby 'enthusiastically' and tells him she 'means it' but Tom contradicts this when he says to Nick 'she doesn't want him.'- they invite him expecting him to decline. This complicated charade of saying the opposite of what you mean in order to be polite mystifies Gatsby, and although Nick, having been brought up amongst these people, his own family he describes as 'prominent, well to do' so he can pick up on these cues, Gatsby says the wrong thing and is then sneered at by his own guests. Fitzgerald depicts this exchange in a way that leads the reader to sympathise with Gatsby, rather than sneer at him with the Sloanes. Just as Gatsby arrives on the steps, the Sloanes 'exchanged a cool nod' before they 'trotted quickly' away. This image of Gatsby standing on the steps of his grand house, watching on in futility, as his invitation and opportunity to spend more time with the husband of his lover slip away down his drive. It occurs just after we hear the story of Gatsby's humble beginnings, and before the second party where the behaviour of the party guests are perceived by Nick to be 'septic'. Through this structure, Fitzgerald encourages the reader to view Gatsby as an innocent, unblemished by the corruption of old money, and simple in his adherence to the basic rules of hospitality- for example, his unease until he has provided drinks for his guests at the beginning of the encounter, contrasts with the way his guests sneer at his misunderstanding at the end.

The Eyes of Dr T J Eckleburg

The eyes of 'god' (owned by Dr T J Eckleburg) who overlook the ash heaps, view the worst behaviour of the characters. When Tom goes to the garage to insult his mistress' husband, and then sneak her away for an afternoon of extra marital seediness, it is seen by Eckleburg. When Gatsby and Daisy plough into Myrtle and leave her dead body in the dust, Eckleburg sees it. In the valley of ash that lay 'half way between West Egg and New York' the 'desolate' land grows 'ashes' instead of 'wheat' in 'grotesque gardens' in a kind of reverse Garden of Eden. Fitzgerald subverts the Bible story by casting the pair out not to go and work in the world, but kills them off instead. This God is not as forgiving.

The billboard is an old advertisement, for an opticians that is now long gone. If God is advertising, then logic follows that for Gatsby and his friends, their religion is capitalism. The advertisement is first referenced in Chapter Two when Nick and Tom go to New York, and Tom 'literally forced' Nick to meet Myrtle. Its 'irises are one yard high' and they 'brood on over the solemn dumping ground'. Through Fitzgerald's characterisation of this advert as a voyeur of the valley, Fitzgerald conveys the idea that the 'eyes' are taking in the behaviour of all those below, and judging those who partake in untoward activity- much like how we think of a god, or a judge. Later, in Chapter Seven, Nick sees 'Doctor T.J.Eckleburg's faded eyes' and they remind him of 'Gatsby's caution about gasoline'. Had Nick not told Tom to stop, then Myrtle would never have seen Tom in the car, and she would never have attempted to stop the car later when Daisy drove the car home. When a grief stricken George tells Michaelis that "God sees everything', Michaelis corrects him, 'That's an advertisement.' This assurance serves to reveal the way Fitzgerald has depicted the society as god-less and lost. Michaelis conversation follows an exchange about George and Myrtle's church attendance, and Michaelis has told George 'You ought to have a church…you must have a church'. Fitzgerald highlights the break between the church and the American people, and in the 1920s church attendance by men in particular had reportedly dropped. Fitzgerald's use of the advertisement as a substitute for God questions the direction America had taken as religious faith diminished.

The Acquisition of money, and the American dream

Nick works with bonds, Tom and Daisy come from money, and Jordan has financial success with her golfing career- something that someone with her wealthy background could pursue because of the freedom money allows. Yet all of them, with the exception of Nick, have some connection with corruption: Gatsby's illegal business deals; Tom's own behaviour in Chicago, and his friend who fell foul of Gatsby and Wolfsheim; Jordan's deceit in her golf match that reached the papers. Nick himself is involved in some duplicity- but this is not money orientated- and when Gatsby offers him an opportunity to make some money, Nick declines, seeing the offer as 'tactlessly' offered in exchange for Nick's help. In this way, Fitzgerald sets Nick apart from the others, and adds to the sense of 'outsider' that surrounds Nick. However, Nick does concede that if this happened at another point it would be 'one of the crises of my life'. Fitzgerald splinters Nick's morality, he rejects the offer, but hints at a time when he may have been tempted- yes, he does ultimately turn it down, but Fitzgerald is further undermining Nick's claim to be 'honest', and critiquing the old money values that pervaded society.

Daisy's appeal to Gatsby is also money orientated: the green light on the dock that encapsulates Gatsby's longing for his wartime sweetheart can also be seen as the symbol for the money that Daisy represents for Gatsby. The money Gatsby makes is not ever accepted by the high society guests- Tom, and the Sloanes, and the guests that Nick notes became brave on Gatsby's liquor and used that courage to make derisory comments about their host. It wouldn't matter how much money Gatsby made, because the money is 'new'. Tom and Daisy are repeatedly described using 'gold', whereas Gatsby and his 'green' imagery represents the new money that will never match up to the 'old money' that society respects so much. In Chapter One, the home of the Buchanans is described as 'glowing now with reflected gold', and in Chapter Seven Nick considers how Daisy is the 'golden girl' with a voice that was 'full of money'.

12. Fitzgerald's use of symbolism

Nature

Pastoral imagery flowers (boom boom) throughout the text. From the obvious Daisy, to the more obscure plum tree in Gatsby's garden. Flowers, and the choice of flowers, gives the text layers of meaning, that illuminating deeper significances that Fitzgerald wanted to direct the reader towards. On the afternoon Gatsby invites Daisy to stay, he fills the home with cut flowers- echoing Daisy's original 'flowering' five years before when they kissed. Here, the flowers can be interpreted as both Gatsby's desire to recreate the past, and also his overwhelming desire to present the very best of things to Daisy to try and impress her. The pear tree comes into importance when Daisy and Nick observe the movie star and the director sitting underneath, with just moonlight between them. Symbolically, the plum tree can symbolise virginity and beauty- and this is matched by the 'orchid' movie star sitting under it- given that orchids symbolise love and in Ancient Greek, virility. However, this beautiful image may appear innocent, but Nick notes that the director has been slowly swooping in to kiss the star on her cheek. The reader could interpret this to echo the relationship between Gatsby and Daisy, everything Gatsby has done has been part of a plan to slowly inch in on Daisy and obtain her love. Alternatively, this could provide a comment on the behaviour of the upper classes- giving the appearance of respectability, whilst actually indulging in lewd and immoral behaviour.

The Green Light

Although this has been touched on elsewhere, it is worth looking at this green light in more detail. The Gatsby, Nick, Daisy triangle of houses connect the characters- and Nick acts as a gateway for Gatsby to reintroduce himself to Daisy. Indeed, Gatsby's nervousness means that this triangle is too close- it is too risky to ask Nick, especially when Jordan informs Gatsby that Nick is a 'particular friend' to Tom, Gatsby wants to 'abandon' the idea. Instead, they settle upon using Jordan as a go between for his go between: Gatsby speaks to Jordan who speaks to Nick, who speaks to Daisy. Fitzgerald is almost ridiculing Gatsby's infantile game play here, by having him use Jordan, as a way to get to Nick, in order to get to Daisy. Just as Gatsby is stuck with the idea of Daisy from five years before, he is also emotionally stunted in terms of his ability to court her. Similarly, the 'single green light' that Nick catches Gatsby staring at the very first time he sees his neighbour (faceless at the time) is the object that Gatsby is forced to transfer his love onto, whilst he cannot obtain Daisy. Later, in Chapter Seven, Gatsby tells Tom that he has loved Daisy 'for five years we…couldn't meet. But both of us loved each other all that time.' The distance between Gatsby and Daisy torments Gatsby, and Fitzgerald uses the green light to symbolise the optimism Gatsby keeps despite the layers of obstacles blurring Gatsby's access to her. Contrast this to Daisy's experience of being without Gatsby: she experienced an episode before the wedding, where she destroyed a letter (we presume from Gatsby) until it was 'pieces of snow'. When Nick meets her, she is disenchanted with life- telling Nick she feels 'pretty cynical about everything'. Was it Gatsby she was yearning for? Fitzgerald provides no clue that it was. Daisy was interested in Gatsby whilst he wore his 'cloak of invisibility' she was oblivious whilst Gatsby wore his soldier's uniform that had allowed him to bypass those obstacles of class during wartime, but with peace and armistice, Gatsby is exposed, and unable to be free to pursue Daisy until he has made himself into the man he thinks he needs to be in order to marry her. Daisy is in the 'twilight universe' where she tried to wait, but faltered, and Jordan describes to Nick her extravagant wedding complete with a pre wedding gift of a pearl necklace worth 'three hundred and fifty dollars.' Fitzgerald appears to be castigating Daisy's impulsiveness, depicting her as shallow and fanciful, tempted by riches and not virtuous in her love. Yet, directly afterwards, we see the other side of Daisy, where she clearly has had second thoughts, and Jordan has been complicit in the orchestration of a marriage to a man wholly unsuitable for her, and who, judging by his infidelities, does not love her. When Nick sees Gatsby and Daisy together, looking at the green light, he notes that one of Gatsby's magical objects has 'diminished by one' when its 'colossal significance…had now vanished forever'. The idea of reality versus fantasy is never able to be equaled for Gatsby, as Nick points out to him, 'you cannot repeat the past' Before now, the green light had felt 'as close as a star to a moon' this celestial imagery continues the characterisation of Daisy as an ethereal being to Gatsby, and continues his impossible worship of her, that as a flawed and damaged human, she could never live up to. Fitzgerald pillories Gatsby: his inability to accept Daisy as she is, his obsession with recreating the past, his insistence of impossible perfection is part of what contributes to his flawed character, and ultimately leads to his downfall.

Driving and Automobiles

Automobiles and driving were still exciting and new modes of transport for most American people. They are symbols of wealth, power, and luxury. All of the characters have in some way made connections to driving, and the connection between their driving abilities and their character: Tom crashes with 'chambermaid' in the car, just shortly after his wedding, epitomising his reckless behaviour, and immoral character. Nick witnesses two drunks who have crashed 'a new coupe' and despite having an 'amputated wheel' in his hands, asks if they have 'run outta gas', and although Nick observes them behaving dreadfully, he yet again fails to step in and help them- merely looks on as an outsider. Jordan is reportedly a lousy driver, and indeed, admits it herself, but places her trust in other people, and feels sure she'll be ok as long as they 'keep out of my way' because 'it takes two to make an accident'. Here Jordan puts trust into Nick, a trust that she later regrets, when she realises he is much more similar to herself than he had led her to believe. Daisy and Gatsby are in the car together when Daisy crashes into Myrtle, 'her life violently extinguished' from the impact of the car. Fitzgerald uses these beast of modernity to exemplify the misuse of society, spoilt by riches. The cars are weaponised, and their power and speed glamourised when Gatsby and Nick 'sped along…With fenders spread like wings [they] scattered light through half Long Island'. Fitzgerald uses cars to demonstrate how the rich have powerful play things, but under appreciate, misuse, and kill with them. Here he is condemning the behaviour of the elite upper classes, and in doing so seems to be criticising the indulgence of a Capitalist and consumerist society.

In Chapter Seven, Gatsby's 'circus wagon', and Tom's 'coupe' in themselves are interesting, insomuch that Gatsby and Tom's car swapping mimics the manner in which they swap partners, and to an extent Tom's attitude towards Daisy that she is just another possession of his to keep or give away. In addition to this, Tom fraudulently claims ownership of Gatsby's car to George Wilson, telling him he 'bought it last week', in a swaggering brag, possibly driven by Tom's determination to 'win' every argument, and to feel powerful and important. To Tom, George is in some way a love rival, being married to the woman he is having an affair with. By feigning ownership to a car driven by a man who he has just realised has been having an affair with his own wife, it serves as a reaffirmation of his masculinity, and a reassurance that his power has not been diminished. This claim is later regretted by Tom, when the lie inadvertently incriminates him in Myrtle's death. Fitzgerald condemns Tom's masculine pride by having the innocuous lie have a greater significance later; the 'careless' attitude of Tom and the wealthier members of society is admonished by Fitzgerald in this lesson in morality.

Gatsby's car provides a physical manifestation of the person Gatsby wished to project of himself when he was 'reborn' on the shore of Lake Superior. Just like the name of the lake that Gatsby stood on, the 'seventeen year old boy' version of Gatsby strove to be 'Superior' to all others, and that included the material possessions. Nick's description of the car is riddled with signs of disapproval of its opulence. His observation that 'Everybody had seen it' smacks of jealousy and resentment. It is 'swollen' and 'monstrous' in shape, with a 'labyrinth of wind-shields'. The use of 'labyrinth' is particularly revealing, as an allusion to the Greek myth of the minotaur. Gatsby's car has a monster inside, and that monster is what will devour Myrtle, and consequently lead to Gatsby's own demise. Fitzgerald's portrayal of the sinister car, foreshadowing its involvement to the later death, condemns Gatsby's flawed character trait of pride. The pride that manifests itself in the obtaining material objects in order to impress Daisy.

Water as a symbol in The Great Gatsby

Water is a significant literary symbol, and writers frequently use it to symbolise moments of truth, rebirth, and sadness. In Christianity, water is used to signify both the 'truth' of Christ, and the moment of baptism when Jesus was submerged in the River Jordan by John the Baptist. This is an act that is still carried out as part of the Christian religion today, and is considered one the most important of the seven sacraments of the church. Water plays a significant part in 'The Great Gatsby', and its symbolism provides much analytical discussion for literary critics.

Essentially, the entire action of the novel is entirely surrounded by water; the Eggs are islands off the East Coast of New York, and therefore Nick's cottage, Gatsby's mansion, and the Buchanan's house are all surrounded by water. The water acts as a barrier between the characters' homes, and their lives in the city. Nick works in New York, and commutes in. Tom travels over to the city to conduct business, and even bumps into Nick and Gatsby there during their lunch with Wolfsheim. The water divides the two worlds, where the behaviour on one side is unnoticed, or ignored by the other. Tom leaves the island to visit his mistress in their secret apartment in Chapter Two, and all of the characters leave the home of the Buchanans' to go to the city and take a hotel suite in Chapter Seven. This crossing the water signifies transgressions in society, where they cross an invisible line that divides morality, and immorality. The ash valley is 'desolate' and 'crumbling' and Tom remarks 'Terrible place' as they leave George Wilson's garage. By constructing the action so that the geography of the novel reflects the behaviour of the characters, Fitzgerald is acknowledging the human fallibility of self delusion. Within Tom there exists a cognitive dissonance, where he knows he is married, and yet has a mistress. Tom claims to love both Daisy and Myrtle, and appears to have compartmentalised the two affairs in his mind. When the line blurs, and Myrtle provokes him by saying Daisy's name, that cognitive dissonance is challenged, and Tom erupts, and 'breaks her nose'.

The day Daisy and Gatsby are reunited the rain is 'pouring' and the rain appears to mirror Gatsby's miserable mood. On Daisy's arrival, her voice was a 'exhilarating ripple' and a 'wild tonic' to the rain. During the following tense and incredibly awkward conversation, the rain continues, and Nick eventually ducks away to leave the two in privacy. When he returns, Gatsby 'literally glowed' and it has 'stopped raining'. On the surface, it may appear that Fitzgerald is simply using water as pathetic fallacy, reflecting the mood of Gatsby who is downcast and uncertain as he awaits to see how his reappearance is received by the object of his affections. Yet underneath, we can see a more interesting Christian ideology being suggested. Gatsby's rain signifies his rebirth, his life has been building to this moment, and something that has previously been dreams is now coming to fruition. The rain washed away his old life, and has confirmed him as a worshipper of Daisy. When they walk towards his home, Daisy 'gleamed' too, and they end the chapter standing 'possessed by intense life' listening to a 'deathless song'. This idea of immortality is signifying her joining the 'church of Gatsby', continuing Fitzgerald's representation of Gatsby as a 'Son of God'. However, there is an element of warning, foreshadowing the ultimate demise of the relationship, when looking out over the water, the pair cannot see the 'green light' due to the 'mist'. This symbolically implies that the water is now coming between Gatsby and his hope for a future with Daisy, and indicating that although they can still speak of the green light, it has 'diminished' now he has obtained Daisy, and must face reality rather than fantasy.

Gatsby himself is cloaked with water imagery: he possesses a 'hydroplane' and is the owner of a 'swimming pool', and when Nick and he first meet, their conversation centres around 'some wet, gray little villages in France'. When Gatsby first meets Dan Cody, it is on the shores on 'Lake Superior' when he is in a 'torn green jersey', Fitzgerald depicts a kind of ragged poor boy, who comes into riches on meeting this eccentric billionaire who takes a liking to Gatsby's smile. Gatsby is always 'reborn' when he encounters water in the novel: his meeting with Cody moves him from 'James Gatz' to 'Jay Gatsby', a 'platonic conception'; with Daisy he is 'an ecstatic patron of perpetual light' signifying Gatsby's movement into a new version of himself; finally at his funeral, Gatsby is buried in 'thick drizzle' and the rain symbolises Gatsby's final transformation into a tragic hero who dies a 'poor-son-of-a-bitch'.

The water also serves as a contrast in Chapter Seven for the 'broiling' heat of the day, and Gatsby's 'coolness'. It is Daisy's observation of Gatsby's 'always looking so cool' that gives away the feelings between them, and it is only in that moment that Tom realises that they are in love. Fitzgerald employs heat as a metaphor for oppression- Nick remarks that 'in this heat every extra gesture was an affront to the common store of life.' Constriction and oppression permeates the entire chapter, as the characters move across the city through the dust valley where we meet Wilson 'hollow eyed' and complaining of his lack of money stopping him taking Myrtle 'West' to 'get away'. We're presented with two more people confined in their position in society, and geographical position in 'relentless beating heat'. Similarly, we then follow the sorry group to the hotel suite where Daisy recalls the moment her constriction began: her wedding to Tom. On that day she recalls 'I was married in the middle of June! Louisville in June! Somebody fainted.' Fitzgerald depicts moments where people are condemned to their fate, and bound up to another person, or place, dressed in heat. This emphasises the opportunity and freedom Gatsby symbolises. In all this heat, he alone is 'cool', and when they look out from the veranda of the Buchanan house, they look over at the horizon, and the water is 'green...stagnant in the heat' just outside the house, but closer to Gatsby's it is 'fresher' 'blue cool' and further away there is a 'scalloped ocean' with 'blessed isles'. This pastoral imagery of 'scallops' and religious allusions of 'blessed' reveals a sense of optimism and hope that is available to them, just away from the toxicity of the home they are in.

13. Aristotle, 'The Tragic Hero', and 'The Great Gatsby'

Aristotle is a pretty important chap, and his book 'Poetics' is pretty much essential reading for every student who is serious about understanding literature. Aristotle was born in Ancient Greece, and lived from 384-322 BC. He is considered the 'Father of Western Philosophy', and he was a student of Plato (another top philosophy fella) and Aristotle himself taught Alexander the Great. Aristotle wrote about many different subjects, and is credited with being one of the main influencing scholars right up until the Renaissance.

Aristotle and tragedy

According to Aristotle, a tragedy must: centre around one serious issue; it uses 'appropriate and pleasurable language' including song; it must be a drama; it must arouse pity and fear for the main character; there must be a cathartic moment where the hero fails and the story reaches a climax.

In order of importance, a tragedy should have: plot, character, thought, diction, melody, and a spectacle.

These ideas can illuminate our understanding of 'The Great Gatsby', as we can see in his composition of the novel many of Aristotle's ideas.

Aristotelean plot and The Great Gatsby

Aristotle's idea that plot must centre around one issue in a tragedy leads us to consider what is the one issue in Fitzgerald's novel- 'The Great Gatsby incorporates ideas about excess, the fragility of the human heart, and the divisions of class in society. But there is one overriding issue that unites all of these smaller ones: the desire to recreate the past. Gatsby's life has been devoted to recapturing the heart of Daisy, and his frustrations when his plan does not pan out as he had hoped. Gatsby is left in Chapter Seven 'watching over nothing', and this futility encapsulates the irrelevance of Gatsby's love.

Aristotle also believed that a plot should contain a moment of discovery: for Gatsby it is this moment in Chapter Seven when Daisy tells him that 'did love [Tom] once' and this shatters the fantasy that Gatsby has been harbouring during the time of their separation. Through Gatsby's shock at the words that 'bite' into him, Fitzgerald reveals the depth of Gatsby's naivety, and the height of his impossible expectations of Daisy. At the start of the novel, Gatsby has blindly believed that Daisy would always love him and only him, despite knowing she had married Tom and had a child with him. Gatsby had deluded himself that Daisy had done all this lovelessly, and in doing so retained a purity in their love. By the end of the novel, Gatsby 'himself didn't believe [a phone call from Daisy] would come...he had lost the old warm world'. Gatsby's discovery means that he ends the novel as a changed man, different from the naive trusting man at the start.

Aristotle is clear that the hero who is 'totally good' can pass from happiness to misery, nor can a 'bad man' pass from misery to happiness, nor can he pass from happiness to misery. These rules exist due to the feelings that it would provoke from the audience. If a person who is totally good befalls an unjust misery, the audience wouldn't pity them- they would be too angry. If a person who is evil is rewarded, again the audience wouldn't feel happiness at their happiness- they would feel it undeserved. Equally, if an evil person 'gets what they deserve' then the audience would not feel pity- rather just satisfaction that they've fallen. Gatsby straddles the line between good and bad, allowing the reader to feel pity. Gatsby's sins are numerous, and complex. Gatsby is clearly swept up in illegal affairs, and lies about it. The friendship between Gatsby and the shady Wolfsheim insinuates that Gatsby is as tangled up as Wolfsheim is in organised crime, on a scale that is as large as having 'fixed the World Series', and portrays Gatsby as someone with weak and dubious morals. When his father considers how Gatsby could have been a 'great man…he'd of helped build up the country' the reader considers this with great scepticism, knowing Gatsby was more concerned about amassing his own personal fortune (albeit for Daisy's approval) rather than improving America as a country. In addition to his business practices, Fitzgerald further confirms Gatsby as a flawed character when he not only pursues another man's wife, but when he also allows that woman to drive away from a scene of a crime. Myrtle's death may not have been Gatsby's fault, but he never returned to the scene to assist the police in their investigation, instead choosing to carry on driving and hiding his car. In this way, Fitzgerald allows us to pity Gatsby when George Wilson shoots him in his swimming pool leaving a 'thin red circle in the water', and we do not feel overly angry, as Gatsby although didn't fully deserve such a dreadful end, had lived a life where this kind of eventuality was always a possibility. Aristotle idea that the best tragedies are about a man who is essentially good, but plagued by a character trait that gets out of hand- known as hamartia. In Gatsby's case, that could be seen as his desire to impress Daisy; although this is not an awful ambition, Gatsby allowed it to overtake his life and cloud all of his judgements. Fitzgerald's choice to have Gatsby shot by George Wilson, rather than a gangster, reveals Fitzgerald's intention that we should view Gatsby as a man who has been brought down by the more noble act of loving the wrong person, rather than dying at the hands of a criminal due to his own criminal activities- which would be much more difficult for a reader to sympathise with.

Aristotle describes the moment when the story reaches its climax and we see the hero experience pain or suffering as 'catharsis', and the experience we have of watching some terrible calamity and experiencing a sense of satisfaction as 'cathartic'. These emotions can explain the popularity of soaps, were we watch people undergo different tortuous miseries with an everyday backdrop. In real life, no one would move into Albert Square, as you could be sure that before the removal men have unpacked all your pots and pans, your long lost adopted daughter will have shown up, been run over by a bus, and then your partner will confess to an affair with your own sibling. And that's before you've found your tin opener. As a modern tragedy, elements of classical tragedy such as catharsis may not be immediately obvious. However, throughout the novel it is possible to identify those enjoyable painful moments, where the slow build up of tensions between Tom, Daisy and Gatsby reach their climax. Chapter Seven in the hotel suite we see the bubbling tensions boil over when Tom finally confronts Gatsby, asking him 'what kind of row are you starting in my house anyhow?' This casual phrasing is possibly part of Tom's determined 'swagger' to cloud any suspicion that he has been emotionally harmed by Daisy's affair. Yet, he is betrayed by his own emotions- the phrasing of 'my house' reveals Tom's deepest fear that Daisy may actually leave him, and in doing so bring down what he considers to be 'my house' by ending their marriage, and Tom's life as he knows it. The audience would enjoy this moment of realisation, as Tom has behaved deplorably since Chapter One, and his affair with Myrtle has been thus far unpunished. To see Tom endure some of the suffering that Daisy has experienced in their five years of marriage allows the audience to experience that alluring catharsis.

According to Aristotle, a tragic hero must be someone noble, or 'larger and better' than the common man. For Shakespeare, this translates as noble Macbeth, or the children of noble households; for Fitzgerald we have 'The Great Gatsby'. In titling his work in this way, Fitzgerald elevates Gatsby above the rest of us, without ever indicating what it was that he did to warrant such a title. Instead of giving Gatsby his nobility from birth, Fitzgerald awards it to Gatsby in his reinvention of himself that occurs before boarding Dan Cody's boat. This new Gatsby gives himself a different heritage- one where his parents were 'wealthy people in the Middle West' whose 'ancestors have all been educated [at Oxford] for many years.' and Gatsby claims to have lived 'like a young rajah' in Europe. This falsified family history is Gatsby's noble heritage, and in this way he rises above the common man, and becomes 'larger and better'. Fitzgerald is acknowledging the ideology of the American Dream that lauds the idea that anyone can make anything of themselves if they simply work hard enough. Gatsby's hard work makes his lie plausible- his grand house and life of excess is indicative of a man raised in privileged surroundings.

14. Feminism and 'The Great Gatsby'

We ask justice, we ask equality, we ask that all civil and political rights that belong to the citizens of the United States be guaranteed to us and our daughters forever. - History of Woman Suffrage (1886)

Fitzgerald wrote 'The Great Gatsby' at a time when only five years earlier women had been granted the vote, birth control advice was beginning to be available, but only to married women, and labour laws restricted times and positions that women could work. They were still ten years away from having an equal minimum wage for men and women, twenty years away from women serving on juries, and fifty years away from legal abortion.

Feminists such as Simone de Beauvoir who wrote 'The Second Sex' in 1949 have had their writings used to help us analyse and interpret literary texts, using their ideas as a springboard to evaluate the role of women in the text. de Beauvoir wrote about the idea that gender is a social construct, and different to biological sex. Valuing women for their looks devalues them as people, and oppresses them into functional roles as wives and mothers. Women are the 'second sex' as they are perceived to be less powerful, less important, and less influential than men. Our society is therefore patriarchal, due to this dominance of men.

'The Great Gatsby' and the dominance of men

Daisy and Gatsby

Although Daisy is the centrifugal force in Gatsby's life, it is in fact his desire to obtain her that drives his love, rather than acceptance of who she is as a person. At the very beginning of their relationship, according to Nick's account of Gatsby's explanation of how the pair met, Gatsby viewed Daisy in terms of her 'value', and this commodification continues when Gatsby is seemingly entranced with the home she lives in so 'beautiful and cool' and the way her wealth was a 'casual' to her, and so exotic to Gatsby. Once reunited following a complex passing of messages, Gatsby is quite overwhelmed with the emotions of seeing Daisy again. Gatsby 'passed visibly through two states...embarrassment and...joy' and then '[entered] a third...wonder'. He had been 'full of the idea' of Daisy and he being together, and when in that moment, she was in his house and they were together, 'he was running down like an overwound clock'. This comparison reveals the depth of Gatsby's infatuation with Daisy, the 'overwound' implying that the whole buildup to that moment was in fact, an excessive and obsessive, and beyond what any reasonable person could be expected to do. By Chapter Seven, the 'wonder' has seemingly rubbed away, leaving Gatsby to 'feel far away' from Daisy, and dwelling on how he can 'repeat the past' permitting the two of them to 'go back to Louisville and be married from [Daisy's] house- just as if it were five years ago.' This inability to view Daisy as a person in her own right, rather than just a symbol of a part of his life he wishes to replicate, reveals the uneven sexual dynamics between the pair. Gatsby's desires dominate the relationship, and Daisy's own wants and needs are only ever superficially services. Gatsby provides Daisy with a 'greenhouse' of flowers, and shows off his 'hulking patent cabinets' with its 'massed...stacks' of clothes, but when faced with Daisy's daughter Pamela, Gatsby is rendered speechless, as if 'he had never really believed her existence before'. This fundamental aspect of Daisy's life is glossed over by Gatsby in his dreaming of Daisy, exemplifying his egocentricity. Fitzgerald depicts Gatsby as a man who loves Daisy on his terms only, and when an alternative is presented to him, it is dismissed. When Daisy is honest and tells Gatsby she loved 'both' Tom and Gatsby,

Gatsby is shocked, but then later dismisses it as 'just personal' and 'she hardly knew what she was saying'. This disregard to Daisy's ideas and feelings echoes the culture at the time, where women were not considered to be capable of the same depth of thought as men. Their work choices were curtailed, voting was contentious as it was believed that women should allow their husbands to vote for them- as encouraged in the pamphlets sent out by the anti-women's suffrage movement. Fitzgerald reflects this ideological standing in his characters, and in doing so can be interpreted as critiquing its misguidance by undermining Gatsby's opinion with the dramatic irony that Daisy was in fact conspiring with Tom, and we later discover the pair have left town.

Daisy and Tom

Daisy's husband Tom is a more obvious symbol for misogyny than gentle Gatsby. Tom's physical presence is an overt embodiment of traditional hyper masculinity. Nick describes Tom as having a body 'cruel body' of 'enormous power' with ''giant pack of muscle' under his clothes. More than this, Tom's attitude is aggressive, competitive, and arrogant; conversationally he engages in overt and covert power plays. Tom tells Nick he has 'never head of' the bond company Nick works for, and this passive aggressive snipe is successful, as Nick felt 'annoyed' at Tom's undermining of his new job. Tom's sexism manifests itself in his attitude towards his wife and what she should be allowed to do- when Tom visits Gatsby's home with the Sloanes, he is told by Gatsby that Daisy knows him. Tom considers Gatsby a 'crazy fish' and tells Nick he 'may be old fashioned in my ideas, but women run around too much these days to suit me.' This reference to Daisy's physical freedom is interesting, given Tom's own 'running around' when he goes to New York and conducts his extra marital affair in the secret apartment that he has rented for Myrtle. Additionally, Daisy is always accompanied by an escort: when she visits Nick, as a relative this is permitted, and when she is left with Gatsby at the end of Chapter Five, Klipsinger is in the house with them, leaving them not quite alone. When the pair steal a 'half-hour' on the steps on Nick's house, Nick remains close by. Daisy does not have the same amount of physical freedom as her husband. This lack of freedom is due to the 1920s expectations of women, and in particular the expectations of women in their role as mothers. The labour laws, and the rules of social etiquette would have meant that Daisy (especially as a wife of a high society husband) would not have been permitted to work outside the home, nor be able to attend social functions without an escort. Daisy's inability to leave Tom could also be interpreted as a consequence of the limitations of women's freedom in 1920. No fault divorce was not yet law, and although divorces were occurring, it was not always a straightforward process, with many Americans needing to travel to more accommodating states in order to have their divorced ratified. These constraints would have pulled Daisy more tightly closer to Tom, as freeing herself from him would not have been a straightforward matter.

Tom and Myrtle

If Tom was controlling towards Daisy, we see a new level of control when it comes to his mistress Myrtle. Myrtle Wilson lives with her husband George Wilson, they are childless and Tom considers George 'so dumb he doesn't know he's alive', and attributes this as the reason he is able to conduct his affair without fear of discovery. Myrtle ascertains that it was Tom who originally approached her whilst she was travelling by train. The entire encounter is described with a type of blurry dreamlike quality, as if Myrtle was merely passive in what occurred, rather than a consenting partner. Tom 'pressed against' her, and she 'didn't hardly know' she was getting into a taxi with him, rather than her next subway. One interpretation could be Fitzgerald was depicting Tom as a dominating sexual aggressor. Tom sees Myrtle, he desires her, he takes her away to have sex with her. The behaviour is reminiscent of that of a caveman, or a commodification of Myrtle- Tom wants to own her, and so he does- she is entirely passive and without agency. Alternatively, this could be an example of Myrtle's need to dissociate herself with the unpleasant reality that she chose to engage in sexual activity with a stranger, and betrayed her own marriage vows. By asserting that she 'hardly knew' she is removing responsibility from herself, to either Tom, or some otherworldly force that pushed the two of them together. This romanticising of the events reveals Myrtle's delusions about the reality of her behaviour: she is having an affair with a married father. However, what prompts Myrtle to delude herself? Societies expectations that women should not desire sexual intercourse, and that their sexual pleasure stems from the excitement of their partner's still permeated society, and the sexologists of the early 20th Century were only just then exploring the science behind the female orgasm and feminine sexuality. Myrtle's framing of events as a passive participant could also be interpreted as a masking of her own sexual desire in order to publicly maintain society's expectations of female behaviour, even if privately she knew the narrative differed. Tom's violence towards Myrtle is described by Nick in a detached and abstract tone. Nick recounts how 'Making a short deft movement, Tom Buchanan broke her nose with his open hand.' The simplicity of the description, devoid of emotion, detail or judgement, is incongruous with the rest of the description in the chapter (and indeed- the whole novel), where we are constantly given Nick's opinion of the events through his detailed accounts of their behaviour. The use of Tom's name serves as a reminder of Tom's privileged background- his name was from a family who were 'enormously wealthy', and that wealth had afforded Tom the best education, and numerous financial opportunities. Yet, here he was, drinking during prohibition, in the secret apartment he rented for his mistress, and committing assault during the course of an argument. Nick's observation of Tom's 'cruel body' foreshadows this event, and Tom's use of his body to control the situation has happened earlier in the chapter when Nick is 'literally forced' when Tom takes him by the elbow and steers him off the train. Fitzgerald uses this hyper masculine character to deride the celebration of overt masculinity, and expose the brutality of such relationships, condemning the violence.

George and Myrtle
Although Tom asserts that George is 'so dumb he doesn't know he's alive', George does eventually realise that his wife has been having an affair, even if he never realised it was with Tom. Compared to Myrtle's almost subservience with Tom, Myrtle is far more forthright with George, and when Nick and Tom visit the garage it is she who orders George to 'Get some chairs, why don't you, so somebody can sit down.' This derisory tone conveys Myrtle's open disapproval of her husband's conduct, the aggressive 'why don't you' implying that George has been negligent in not doing so already, and the unspecific 'so somebody' implies that by having not already provided chairs, he has been in some way unaccommodating for the visitors, depriving them of the basic need to sit. George's instance compliance subverts the expected gender roles, and contrasts their home life with the Buchanans, where Tom never takes orders from Daisy, and even her teasing about his 'deep books with long words' is met with Tom's 'impatient' glance. These two occurrences take place next to each other, and by structuring these chapters side by side, Fitzgerald invites the reader to compare the parallels of Tom's public life with his private one. Publicly, Tom maintains a level of authority over his wife, but privately, he engages in an illicit affair with a woman whose husband has no authority over her. Fitzgerald acknowledges the changing gender dynamics through these alternative representations of domesticity, and seems to be questioning what the male role is in the modern world. This idea is further explored in Chapter Eight, following Myrtle's death, George and Michaelis are discussing the marriage, and the argument the previous night. Michaelis attempts to

'distract' George by questioning him about 'church', 'children' and the length of their marriage. This focus upon the traditional components of marriage reveals the shallowness of George and Myrtle's union. Fitzgerald could be using the voice of Michaelis to draw the reader's attention to the perils of the 'godless' society of the 1920s, and the consequences of abandoning more traditional values- such as going to church and being open to children. However, Tom and Daisy's child Pamela did nothing to dissuade Tom from his philandering, and indeed, we learn from Daisy that Tom was 'god knows where' even at her birth, implying that even on that important occasion he was out with other women. Fitzgerald seems to be insinuating that the morals of the Americans have been corrupted, regardless of their position in society, or attempts to adhere to traditional values. Fitzgerald paints a bleak portrait of love, depicting a society where sadness is everywhere.

In addition to this, Fitzgerald also uses the position of domestic staff to explore the position of women in this privileged society. Nick's detached tone when describing his 'Finnish Woman' whom he lists along with the dog and car when listing his property. This casual commodification is indicative of not only the position of women in society, but also the casual racism of classifying a person by the nationality, and additionally the attitude towards the immigrant working poor by the wealthy Americans. Nick never gives the reader any indication that he considers the woman as a person unto herself, and instead describes her as an oddity that lives to serve him, informing the reader she 'made my bed and cooked breakfast and muttered Finnish wisdom to herself over the electric stove.' The focus on both her domestic duties, and repetition of her nationality demonstrates the servitude of women of a working class.

Gender and Identity in 'The Great Gatsby'

The sexologists of the early 20th Century were writing about the emergence of 'sexual inversion' where women appeared to be adopting typically masculine traits, and behaving in ways that was considered subversive and for some conservatives, obscene. In 1908 Havelock Ellis published 'Studies in the Psychology of Sex: Sexual Inversion' where Ellis describes the practices of homosexual females, and analyses the behaviour of 'mannish woman'. The American sexual politics of the early 20th Century were concerned with the emergence of homosexual behaviour, and the idea of female sexual pleasure. Conservative American society was rocked by the shock of not just the idea that women could enjoy sex, but that people of the same sex could be engaged in relationships.

Fitzgerald's depiction of Jordan Baker is an intriguing character insomuch that her ambiguity, and androgyny sets her apart from the other characters. The choice of 'Jordan' as a first name is a deliberate nod to her masculinity, and although today it is considered to be a unisex name, using social security records we can see there is no record of its use as a female name in America until 1978. Every single description of Jordan contains the word 'jaunty' in some form. 'Jaunty' implies confidence- a quality that is typically associated with masculinity, rather than femininity. Nick is more focused on Jordan's more masculine attributes, noting the way she 'wore her evening-dress, all her dresses, like sports clothes' the symbolic implications of the 'dress' as the epitome of the feminine- the piece of clothing then thought to belong to a woman, and only a woman, reveals Nick's consideration of Jordan as a rejection of traditional femininity. Nick is attracted to Jordan, and engages in a relationship with her, so therefore by describing Jordan as such, Fitzgerald is making a comment upon the new kind of woman that the modern world was creating: one that could be athletic, independent, and in control of her own sexuality. Jordan's name also has significance in terms of its closeness to Josephine Baker, the notorious sexually liberal entertainer, who moved to Europe and associated with famous writers and painters (friends of Fitzgerald) and commanded high fees for her performances. By connecting these two women, Fitzgerald could be seen to be reflecting the women of the Jazz Age who were shocking the world with their sexual freedom. Jordan's sexuality is also hinted at when Nick comments that she begun lying young in order to 'satisfy the demands of her hard, jaunty body'. There is an insinuation that those 'demands' are in some way subversive, or controversial, given Jordan's need to lie to meet the demand. This observation of Nick's echoes Jordan's claims she prefers large parties for their 'intimacy', intimating her predilection for opportunities to speak confidentially, and conduct herself in a way that may not be permitted so openly; Jordan could be argued to be hiding her sexual preferences in plain sight. In this way, Fitzgerald could be interpreted as pairing Jordan and Tom together as two people who both subvert societal norms using their position in high society as a veneer of respectability to hide their behaviour.

Women in 'The Great Gatsby'

Through the structure of first person narration, we literally have the 'male gaze' throughout the text. In feminist theory, the male gaze describes the way events and people are viewed through a masculine and heterosexual point of view. Nick provides an interesting perspective on the women in the novel. When Nick first sees Jordan and Daisy in Chapter One, he describes them upon 'an enormous couch…both in white' in describes the fabric of their dresses as 'rippling and fluttering'. In this paragraph, Nick's description of the couch, and the two women upon it, are described as if they were one and the same. This signifies how Nick fails to see Daisy and Jordan as people, but rather decoration within the house. The 'white' of their dresses could be suggested to be a symbol of purity, but it could also be interpreted as Fitzgerald's signaling of their 'uniform' of purity. Daisy and Jordan both wear white in Chapter One, and also Chapter Seven, when Daisy's daughter, Pamela remarks 'Aunty Jordan's got on a white dress too'. The women dress themselves in white to outwardly signal their virtue, rather than being intrinsically virtuous in themselves. This need for women to publicly avoid scandal, and to be seen to be virtuous is echoed in Tom's attitude towards Daisy's 'run[ning] around too much to suit [him]', when he himself was caught in a car with a 'chambermaid' shortly after his wedding, and he 'sauntered about' in 'popular restaurants' with his mistress, flagrantly breaking his marriage vows. Fitzgerald contrasts these expectations for men and women, and seems to be criticising a society where women are held to different standards to men. There is a hypocrisy of signaling virtue in white, whilst kissing your lover with your husband is in the other room. Daisy's lack of virtue is also apparent when asked to attend a social engagement without her husband, and simply asks 'Who is Tom?' and colludes with the secrecy without question. Additionally, Nick describes the faces of women as 'blurry' at various points in the novel; Catherine, Myrtle's sister is described as having 'blurred air' to her face, having plucked out and then redrawn on her eyebrows. Additionally, Jordan and Daisy's conversation is viewed as 'inconsequential banter' and that they both 'talked at once'. This blurring of their voices, and the blurred faces contribute to Fitzgerald's portrayal of Nick having a 'fuzzy' and unclear view of women. They exist alongside him, but they are not what interests him.

At Gatsby's parties, the female guests serve as both the decoration and entertainment, the girls in yellow dresses perform 'a baby act in costume', and Nick watches as 'old men push young girls in graceless circles'. This subservience of women extends to the vignettes we are presented with as the guests exit: 'wayward' men stay, with one keen to speak to a 'young actress' with a 'curious intensity', whilst his wife 'broke down'. Two drunk women complain about leaving so early to their sober husbands, before there was a 'struggle' and the husbands carry the women off into the night. These alcohol fueled scenes at the party do seem to be presenting women as there for the enjoyment of men, even at the second party when Daisy and Nick watch the film director slowly lean in to kiss the actress underneath the 'white plum tree' in the 'moonlight', the males are ultimately the ones in control. Fitzgerald mirrors the 1920s patriarchal society, where women's growing rights are met with resistance at every stage. Women were still believed to exist for the enjoyment of men, and although we see women exhibiting some agency, the overwhelming impression is that it will always be the male who ultimately controls the situation.

15. Marxism and 'The Great Gatsby'

'It would have been much better that instead of writing a lot about capital, Karl had made a lot of it.' - Karl Marx's Mother

Karl Marx did indeed write a lot about capital and Capitalism. Capital meaning money, and capitalism (as discussed in the earlier chapter) the pursuit of profit by individuals, rather than the state. Karl Marx, along with others, wrote many political and economic theories, and we now refer to 'Marxism' and 'Marxist' when we discuss the theory that **society is capitalist** because it is focused on making profit for individuals, not all the people. The **working class (proletariat)** make money for the **upper classes (bourgeoisie)** and it is the upper classes who are in control. These two classes are in conflict, as the upper classes exploit the working classes for their own benefit.

In 'The Great Gatsby' Fitzgerald splits the wealthy geographically: we have the East and West Eggs, the ash valley, and the road that connects them. Nick works, but he is not what we would consider working class, although he is obviously less wealthy than the Buchanans. Daisy and Tom clearly represent the bourgeoisie, and their easy wealth allows the exploitation of the working class. Tom exploits George Wilson's poverty when he dangles the sale of his car, threatening to 'sell it somewhere else' when George dares to complain about the speed at which the sale is moving. Fitzgerald uses the car sale to symbolise the power and authority Tom has over George, and when George discovers Myrtle's affair, Tom finally concedes 'I'll let you have that car', prompted by guilt for his own part in George's misery. Later, when George is by the roadside following the crash, Tom lies to George, using the car again to give his lie credibility, telling him he 'was bringing [George] the blue coupe' to distract from his real motivation for stopping. In this way, we see George at the mercy of the Buchanans, his weakness stemming from his working-class roots, and the ease with which Tom can exploit him due to his own elevated position in society.

The East and The West

Nick moves east to make money at the beginning of the novel, and then by the end has decided that he was 'subtly unadaptable to Eastern life' and has decided to move back west. The east has provided Nick with the opportunity to pursue his career in bonds, and Tom asserts that he'd 'be a god damned fool to live anywhere else.' The vehemence in his tone hints not only at the past misdemeanours in Chicago, but Tom is also sneering at the 'fool' who lives for something other than the pursuit of money. This superiority confirms Tom's position as a member of the bourgeoisie- one who is rich, and happy to exploit others to remain so. Nick's confusing position is muddied by the acknowledgement of his own family history. His 'grand-father's brother...sent a substitute to the Civil War', a practice common with the implementation of the Enrolment Act (also known as draft laws) in 1863 which allowed the wealthy pay $300 to avoid service but risk being drafted later, or sending a substitute, which could cost up to $1000 but avoid service for the duration of the war. This capitalist behaviour exemplifies to bourgeois attitude that Marx wrote about in 'The Communist Manifesto', where the proletariate are commodified by the bourgeois. Nick's family's fortune was built on the back of one man's ability to 'purchase' another man's life. Fitzgerald's condemnation of this practice is evident in the deliberate connection between Nick and this great uncle to whom Nick has a close resemblance, and there is a 'hard-boiled painting' of him in his family home, serving as an echo to the framed photograph of Dan Cody Gatsby hangs in his. In addition to this, Nick's detached tone when describing his 'Finnish Woman' whom he lists along with the dog and car in his list of property. This casual commodification is both indicative of the casual racism of classifying a person by the nationality, and also the attitude towards the immigrant working poor by the wealthy Americans. Nick never gives the reader any indication that he considers the woman as a person unto herself, and instead describes her as an oddity that lives to serve him, informing the reader she 'made my bed and cooked breakfast and muttered Finnish wisdom to herself over the electric stove.' When Nick agrees to host the Daisy and Gatsby reunion, Nick realises he had 'forgotten to tell my Finn', and he drives into the village to fetch her back. The focus on both her domestic duties, and repetition of her nationality, and the use of the possessive pronoun 'my' demonstrates Nick's lack of concern of her as a person, and the position of the working poor as powerless proletariat.

Despite Nick's position of advantage, he adopts a derisory tone when describing the luxuries afforded his friends, when describing the indulgence of Gatsby's parties, he coolly notes that the orange juicer could 'extract the juice of two hundred oranges…if a little button was pressed two hundred times by a butler's thumb.' This repetition of 'two hundred' conveys Nick's scepticism of the usefulness of such a contraption, expressing his doubt that such an invention serves any purpose other than to make more work for the 'butler' who must work the machine. The inclusion of the butler reminds the reader of the reliance of staff that the bourgeois characters have; Tom and Daisy also employ a nanny for their daughter, whom Nick describes as a 'freshly laundered nurse'. This patronising description further compounds the presentation of the richer characters considering those that work for them as faintly amusing curiosities, that are somehow existing in lives that merely serve to assist the wealthy. Fitzgerald choice to include these descriptions implies an unease with these attitudes, and highlights them through Nick's narration.

The personal whims of the bourgeoisie adversely impact upon the lives of the proletariat, and despite not being directly involved in the argument that occurs in Chapter Seven, Myrtle is the one to lose her life when she steps out into the road expecting to see Tom, and instead finding Gatsby and Daisy driving straight at her. George is innocently tangled up in the dramas between Gatsby and the Buchanans, and yet it is he who lies dead in the orchard by the swimming pool. Nick's condemnation of this behaviour rings hollow; he claims Daisy and Tom 'smashed things up and then retreated back into their money' condemning their duplicity at the crime scene, and then retreat leave East Egg in the aftermath to avoid conviction and scandal. On the surface, Nick can be seen as a more honest person, insomuch that he stays and cares for Gatsby in his death, and arranges the funeral attempting to honour the life of a man whom no one wants to know now that he can provide no more hospitality to them. And yet underneath we see Nick is not so different himself, when he was at the crime scene, he colludes with Tom and follows his suggestion to leave. Similarly to Tom, he also eventually leaves the east, and returns west by the end of the novel. Fitzgerald reveals how although how it is true for all people that we prefer to think of the best of ourselves, even when we can easily identify the same faults in others. Although Nick would prefer to consider himself different to the other bourgeois characters, he is in fact not so very different after all.

Q Find all references to the 'staff' in the novel. Compare their descriptions. What do you notice about what they have in common?

Q Nick, Daisy and Gatsby walk through 'Marie Antoinette music-rooms' in Chapter Five. What connection does Marie Antoinette have to Capitalism, Marxism, and the bourgeoisie?

Q What has happened to Gatsby's mansion by the end of the novel? Find quotations to describe its appearance, and consider how this links to Marx's ideas.

16. Greek allusions

The Greek Gatsby - Greek Mythology in The Great Gatsby

From Shakespeare, to Dickens, to Baz Lurhman's 'Moulin Rouge', the Greek Myths are alluded to across all types of literature, theatre and film. References to the heroes, gods and goddesses from the Greek myths are frequently woven into our stories to give an extra layer of meaning to the narrative. These allusions allow us to analyse the events in a slightly different way, or give us an alternative interpretation of the writer's intentions.

A super quick who's who in Greek Mythology

Zeus

This is the guy who is in charge of all the Olympian Gods. He overthrew his father, and then drew lots with his brothers Poseidon and Hades to decide who would replace their dad. Zeus won, so he was in charge (plus the sky and thunderbolts- handy), Poseidon ruled the sea, and Hades the underworld.

Zeus was an amorous type, and was always going about and impregnating various mortals. He was married to Hera (who was his wife AND sister), and he was always upsetting her with his many affairs.

Zeus' children were: Athena, Apollo, Artemis, Hermes, Persephone, Dionysus, Perseus, Heracles, Helen of Troy, Minos, and the Muses.

Athena

Athena was not born in a normal way- she appeared from Zeus' forehead. Fully formed and wearing armour. Athena is the goddess of intelligent activity, and Zeus' favourite.

Apollo

Apollo was the son of Zeus and Leto (a goddess Zeus had impregnated before marrying Hera) and he had a twin brother called Artemis. Apollo was the god of light, and amongst other important tasks, it was him who pulled the sun across the sky in his chariot every day. Thanks for that.

In The Great Gatsby, we can see Fitzgerald alluding to some of the famous Greek myths...

Gatsby as Apollo

Apollo was one of the more important gods, and he pops up in both Greek and Roman mythology; he is a lucky so and so, and considered to be the god of all kinds of stuff- music, the sun, poetry, prophecy...but mostly the sun. Apollo is probably best known for throwing big parties, playing a Lyre (he invented it himself- nice) and having muses dance around him. Does this sort of behaviour sound familiar? Gatsby could be seen as a modern-day Apollo.

However, where do we really draw the connection between the two? Well, Fitzgerald leaves us a clue in Wolfsheim's firm 'The Swastika Holding Company'. The swastika is the symbol for the sun; when Hitler adopted it for the Nazi party, he was evoking a different sun god- Odin of the Valkyries. However, when Fitzgerald uses it, he is drawing a connection to Apollo, the sun god.

Throughout the novel, Gatsby is described in reference to light: his smile is 'radiant', his car is 'bright with nickel' (chapter four), and his parties had guests come and go 'like moths', implying that Gatsby and his home are the flame (chapter three). However, when Gatsby becomes his most bright is when he is in contact with Daisy. In chapter five, Gatsby's brightness goes into overdrive.

The chapter opens with Nick commenting that a party at Gatsby's house was 'blazing with light', and it looks 'unreal'. Gatsby and Daisy's awkward and emotionally charged meeting seems to cause Gatsby to blaze further, and Nick describes him as an 'ecstatic patron of recurrent light'. This idea of eternity and perpetual light echoes the mythological image of Gatsby as Apollo. From meeting Daisy, Gatsby seems to have become more godlike, and now Nick claims he 'literally glowed…a new wellbeing radiated from him and filled the little room.'. After being reunited with Gatsby, we now have Daisy, and she is also glowing, as the 'brass buttons on her dress gleamed in the sunlight.'. Together, these two are lighting up the novel in Apollo-style brightness.

So what is Fitzgerald trying to say with all this sunlight and Greek mythology? If Gatsby is a modern Apollo, what can we the reader conclude from that?

Consider the parties Apollo threw: his muses dancing around him whilst he played his Lyre. Gatsby throws these similar parties, but does anyone know who he is? This god of the Jazz age is now hosting his parties in almost anonymity, all in the pursuit of a woman he is too nervous to approach, and with muses who openly hold him in contempt. At the very end of the novel when Carraway is calling the muse-party goers to attend the funeral, he finds little interest. Indeed, one insinuates Gatsby's death is his own fault, and Carraway remembers he 'used to sneer most bitterly at Gatsby on the courage of Gatsby's liquor.'. This is no Grecian golden age; modern America is riddled with insincerity, and self-interest.

In your essay you might use this to analyse Gatsby and say something like:

Fitzgerald alludes to the Greek God Apollo in his depiction of Gatsby as a god of light and party going Fitzgerald is creating a picture of a god who has no sincerity, no truth, and no morality. Gatsby's Apollo depiction foreshadows his death, and the betrayal of all those that were attracted to the wealth without ever knowing the man.

Q Find all references to Gatsby's car and house in the novel. Collect quotations that link to the theme of light, and consider how they change over the course of the novel.

Q When Gatsby dies, Carraway speculates on Gatsby's last thoughts…what were they? How can you connect this to the idea of Gatsby as Apollo, and the importance of light?

Gatsby as Athena

Gatsby and Athena have an important tie: both were created spontaneously. Athena came fully formed from Zeus' forehead, and Gatsby (or James Gatz) had parents, but he 'had never really accepted them', and Carraway tells us that 'Jay Gatsby...sprang from his Platonic conception of himself. He was a son of God'. This immaculate conception is probably more important when considering what it tells us about the psychology of Gatsby: here is a man who cannot except his own parents, and his own history. Instead, he invents one to suit himself.

Gatsby's rejection of his father becomes all the more tragic when at his death, it is only his father, Nick, and Owl Eyes that attend the funeral. Gatsby may have seen himself as an Athena, born of a God from a platonic conception, but the reality is that he was born and died James Gatz- an ordinary man. This gap between how we see ourselves, and how others see us is echoed again in Nick Carraway: insists that he is honest, as we discover his unreliability as a narrator.

Q Consider Gatsby's language when he speaks to Nick about his past in chapter four. In what way does Gatsby rely upon this version of history where he has come from nothing?

Q Why are Gatsby's origins important when we consider Fitzgerald's ideas regarding the American Dream?

Gatsby as Icarus

Icarus wasn't a god, he was the son of the man who built the labyrinth, Daedalus. In order to escape a tower, Icarus and Daedalus flew away on wings Daedalus had built. Despite being warned not to by his father, Icarus flew too close to the sun, and the heat melted his artificial wings, and he plunged to his watery death below.

The Gatsby-Icarus allusion pops up when Gatsby's dream to be with Daisy almost comes to fruition in chapter seven: Daisy tells Tom she wants to marry Gatsby, and Gatsby and Daisy drive off together (albeit under Tom's instruction, and his stubborn belief that Daisy would never leave him for a man like Gatsby).

From chapter seven there are a series of mistaken identities: Myrtle believes Tom is driving the car, Daisy lets Gatsby tell people he was driving the car, and then later Tom misleading Mr Wilson into believing it was Gatsby having an affair with Myrtle. Although Myrtle is the initial victim of the crash, it is Gatsby himself who plunges into the water, not of the Aegean sea, but of his own swimming pool, as a consequence of the misjudged flying too close to the sun.

Gatsby's yellow car 'with fenders spread like wings' crashes into Myrtle; this Icarus style tragedy leads us to conclude that Gatsby has tried too hard, he flew too close to the sun, and consequentially failed. Fitzgerald's disillusionment with the American Dream is illustrated perfectly here: Gatsby made himself. He came from nothing, and then acquired all of the expected commodities to signal success. His 'new money' did not matter, and the 'old' families like the Buchanan's may not like it, but he succeeded anyway. However, Gatsby flew too high, and paid for it with his life.

Fitzgerald puts Daisy in the clouds elsewhere in the novel- in chapter five she calls Gatsby to a window to look at 'pink clouds' that she wants to 'push [him] around' in. Daisy is the ever ethereal, always out of reach object of Gatsby's desires. Icarus is not a tragic hero, but instead his death serves as a morality tale to not choose the 'golden path'. This pieces together with Gatsby's own mistakes- he would have done well to take heed of the inscription at the temple of Apollo in Delphi: 'Nothing in Excess'.

Daisy is Gatsby's sun. He flew too close, and too high, and when his yellow car crashed, so did his chance to be with her.

Q Piece together the information about the crash from the different characters. Make a note of which character gives which piece of information.

Q Re-read chapter seven, and make a list of all of the clues that the crash is going to happen.

Q Consider how likely it is that Daisy is going to leave Tom. What evidence can you find that Gatsby's dream is not going to come true?

Daisy as a Siren

The sirens were beautiful women who enticed sailors with their enchanting voices, and then destroyed them, or let them die at sea. Odysseus famously tied himself to the mast and stuffed up the ears of his sailors so he would be able to hear the voices of the sirens, but be stopped from acting upon the urge to jump ship. Daisy is our beautiful siren with her special voice.

Consider these quotations:

'The exhilarating ripple of her voice was a wild tonic in the rain.' (chapter five)

'Her voice is full of money' (chapter seven)

What is Fitzgerald suggesting about Daisy, and the way her voice makes others feel?

It is a consequence of being under Daisy's spell, just like those unfortunate sailors, that means Gatsby dies in the water of his monogrammed swimming pool.

The dark side of Daisy is siren-esque too. She is duplicitous, quickly slipping into an affair with Gatsby, and makes a cuckold of her husband. When the affair is seemingly exposed in chapter seven, Daisy's uncertainty leads the reader to not truly believe she is capable of sticking to her word and leaving Tom. Daisy entices Gatsby, puts him under a spell, and then disappears again.

Even the green light on the dock can be interpreted as a Siren sign. This light (by the water) calls to Gatsby, and puts him under a spell. Just like the mythical Sirens, Daisy has Gatsby mesmerised by her, and calls him to her across the water with her otherworldly powers.

Q Find all the quotations that link Daisy to water (including rain).

Q Consider the quotations regarding the green light, and Daisy's power over Gatsby.

Q Re-read the flashback to Daisy and Gatsby's kiss. To what extent does Fitzgerald imply Gatsby is under her spell?

The Blind Prophet

You may have heard of the 'blind prophet' or be familiar with the literary idea that those who are blind have instead a 'sixth sense' of intuition. The original blind prophet was Teiresias, and he was the prophet of Apollo (ah ha!). He accidentally saw Athena in the nip, and so Athena responded in an entirely reasonable manner: she blinded him. Teiresias' mother got involved, and persuaded feisty Athena to relent a little…Teiresias was still blind, but Athena gave him a 'second sight' to soften the blow.

Our blind prophet in Gatsby isn't quite blind, but needing glasses and getting blind drunk is close enough. It's also worth noting that Athena sometimes appeared as an owl. At Gatsby's party, Owl Eyes first meets Carraway and Baker in Gatsby's library.

"'See!" he cried triumphantly. It's a bona-fide piece of printed matter. It fooled me. This fella's a real Belasco. It's a triumph. What thoroughness! What realism! Knew when to stop, too- didn't cut the pages. But what do you want? What do you expect?"'

Owl Eye's joy that the books are real, but not cut, suggests to the reader that he knows what Gatsby is- a fake. But a good one. There is authenticity in his duplicity. Gatsby has acquired money through dubious means, but he has done it for pure reasons- love. In Gatsby's lies there are elements of truth; he did go to Oxford and he did inherit money. It is just that he only stayed five months, and he was never able to collect the money he inherited. If we take Owl Eyes to be a prophetical character, we can then see his words as truth. Gatsby may be fake, but he is a real fake; and to expect anything more is unreasonable.

The comparison to 'Belasco' is an interesting one: David Belasco was a successful theatre producer, known for his detailed set design. In this way, Fitzgerald is foreshadowing the later reveal of Gatsby as a showman- the stage he has dressed to entice Daisy back into his life. Nick Carraway is yet to find this out, and at this stage still thinks of Gatsby as an eccentric and indulgent party goer.

Owl Eyes sees and admires this 'realism' in Gatsby, when other 'muses' or partygoers are too busy drinking his liquor. Other guests speculate on Gatsby's authenticity, but Owl Eyes is able to ascertain his fraudulence, and the depth of his fraudulence, from Gatsby's library. Owl Eyes sees the truth first. At the end of the novel, it is Owl Eyes who is the sole mourner to join Nick Carraway and Gatsby's father for Gatsby's funeral. Owl Eyes appears out of the rain, and Nick notes 'I don't know how he knew about the funeral' but our prophetic Owl Eyes just knew, reconfirming our interpretation of Owl Eyes as a character who is able to foretell the future.

Q Owl Eyes went to the library to sober up, having been drunk for a week. In what way could you say he was the same as the other party goers?

Read further: Owl Eyes is impressed that Gatsby has not cut the books. In the 1920s, books were bought 'uncut' and then the edges of the pages cut when you read them. Sometimes this is called 'deckle edging', and it was unavoidable until advancements in technology and paper printing meant they changed the way books

were manufactured. Search online to find photographs and videos of deckle edged books.

Q If the books were uncut, what does this mean Gatsby hasn't done? Why would this impress Owl Eyes? How could you connect this to Gatsby's comments about Oxford in chapter seven?

17. Sample question and answer

Example Essay Answer

Assessment Objectives

AO1 Articulate creative, informed and relevant responses to literary texts, using appropriate terminology and concepts, and coherent, accurate written expression.

AO2 Demonstrate detailed critical understanding in analysing the ways in which structure, form and language shape meanings in literary texts.

AO3 Explore connections or comparisons between different literary texts, informed by interpretations of other readers.

AO4 Demonstrate understanding of the significance and influence of the contexts in which literary texts are written and received.

Q How far do you agree with the view that Fitzgerald presents Gatsby's life as pitiful rather than inspiring?

Gatsby in many ways seems to be an enviable character: he lives in a beautiful home, he throws lavish parties that are attended by hundreds of people, and he has numerous desirable material possessions. However, so much of his life is pitiful.

Gatsby is a tragic hero whose failure is foreshadowed throughout the novel. Fitzgerald depiction of Gatsby alludes to the Greek god Apollo because he throws his parties, and orchestrates the opulence, with the 'muse' partygoers surrounding him. Like the sun god, everything about Gatsby is bright, from his 'radiant' smile, to his 'blazing' home. However, these parties are all tinged with sadness, as they only exist to attract the attentions of a woman who he projects his love onto, but actually does not understand. Gatsby as a Jazz age Apollo cuts a pathetic figure; he is anonymous amongst the crowds, and his own guests speculate upon his illegal business activities.

Gatsby is at his most pitiful when he and Daisy drive his car with its 'fenders spread like wings' into Myrtle. All of the dark warnings about the dangers of driving that run through the novel come true, with Myrtle's death, and ultimately Gatsby's own murder. Here, Fitzgerald echoes Icarus' fall, as Gatsby has overreached, and societal expectations of class prevent him from being with Daisy.

Example Essay Question and Answer

Q At the heart of the tragic experience is a powerful sense of hope. To what extent do you agree?

Hope and the tragic experience are irreversibly intertwined: without hope, then loss cannot feel tragic, and unless you've experienced loss, then you cannot understand what it means to hope for change. The notion that hope lies at the centre of the tragic experience, and is in fact its driving force, can absolutely be supported by the characters and events of Fitzgerald's 'The Great Gatsby'. Through his creation of a world where every man and woman is hoping for something more, and yet never achieving fulfilment, Fitzgerald questions whether man's tragic experience is caused by external factors, or if it is intrinsic to his very being.

Gatsby and Daisy are reunited after a seemingly tortured separation, during which neither was happy, and both seemed to be hoping for some elevation from their unhappy situations. Gatsby had been 'full of for so long' and 'dreamed right through to the end' sits right at the heart of the text in terms of structure and its 'colossal vitality' can certainly be seen to be the optimistic desire which drives the plot. In addition to this, Miller's suggestion in 'Tragedy and the Common Man' that 'the possibility of victory must be present' in order for a play to evoke truly tragic feelings of catharsis is certainly evident in their reunion, where the tone of the text shifts from melancholic to 'elemental and profound'. For a time, the reader, just like Gatsby, dares to hope that there will be happiness in their ending, and that Gatsby and Daisy will find completion in each other.

Although Gatsby appears at times almost crippled with a lack of self-belief, he is paradoxically also profoundly hopeful. The imagery of 'the green light' provides the reader with a perfect example of Gatsby's 'extraordinary gift for hope'. The green light at the end of the dock is 'minute and far away', and only available to him via the purchase of an expensive house, and yet it is still an 'enchanted object' to him, and whilst Daisy is merely a dream and out of reach, it becomes his focus of his desires. The purchase of the expensive house, and the rest of Gatsby's indulgent luxuries all form part of the tragic magnificence, which is central to the plot. Gatsby's 'entire caravansary' that he created in order to 'win' Daisy comprises of his 'gorgeous car' and 'colossal affair' of a house. Gatsby, aware of his disadvantaged social status, is attempting to reverse his fortunes by becoming the man that Daisy could see as her social equal. If it is the hope that Daisy will admit that 'in her heart she never loved anyone but' Gatsby that is symbolised in the green light, it can certainly be argued that hope sits at the heart of the tragic experience.

Daisy's doomed rival, Myrtle, acts as a parallel for Gatsby's hope: where Gatsby hopes that Daisy will leave Tom, Myrtle hopes that Tom will leave Daisy. Fitzgerald repeatedly uses the word 'vitality' in his descriptions of Myrtle. In doing so, he depicts a woman who stands out from the backdrop of hopelessness of the valley of ashes where 'ash grey men move dimly and already crumbling'. When she describes her hope that the Buchanan's marriage will end and she and Tom will 'go West for a while until is all blows over' this hope is central to her tragic escape from the garage where she 'rushed out into the dark, waving her hands and shouting' and results in the first of a series of deaths which make up the 'holocaust' that ends the novel on a suitably tragic tone. It may have been hope that drove Myrtle to run towards Gatsby's car, Fitzgerald contrasts this with his description of her death full of melancholy and pessimism. When 'her which dark blood' mingles with the ash of the valley that she dreamed of escaping but never could, Fitzgerald appears to be making a social comment upon the futility of hope and optimism for the lower classes in 1920s America. The Tom Buchanan offered her hope, but without sincerity; she was sold a dream that would never have a delivery date.

Gatsby's tragic murder, a result of Tom's cowardice, and Daisy's lack of conviction, coupled with the paltry attendance at Gatsby's funeral, drives the novel towards a sombre ending. When Nick arranges Gatsby's funeral, he is greatly distressed that he is unable to 'get anyone' despite his attempt to persuade Gatsby's friends and business contacts to come. Yet, instead of concluding the novel with reminders of the tragedy, Fitzgerald deliberately contracts an optimistic tone, albeit a cautious one. In the novel's concluding paragraphs, we are reminded again of the 'green light' and Nick's fictive biography describes how 'tomorrow we will run faster, stretch out our arms further…And one fine morning - '. There is an unspoken promise in the use of the unfinished sentence and despite the death of the protagonist, and Nick's retreat back to the West, Fitzgerald ends the text with a sense of optimism and catharsis.

Highlight – references to the tragic genre

      Discussion of method

      Textual support

      Argument in line with the task

      Relevant and integrated terminology

      Relevant and integrated context

      Analysis/evaluation of effects

Examiner comment:

This answer offers an immediate and genuinely personal engagement with the text and the genre, and perhaps most importantly with the task. It is demonstrative from the first paragraph that the student has a detailed understanding of the text and the genre and also that they are able to interpret the question in all of its parts and offer a reasoned and contextualised argument. The student's choices for discussion are thoughtfully chosen and carefully organised, both within paragraphs and as a complete essay. Key words such as 'hope' and 'tragic experience' are clearly flagged up in topic sentences which inform the examiner what the individual focus of each paragraph will be, without losing sight of the terms for debate. There is a sustained attention to narrative method, and therefore a clear sense that the students understand Fitzgerald's control over the narrative. The student does not assume to assert what Fitzgerald was thinking when he constructed characters and events, but is confident enough to offer up an interpretation of the impact of his narrative choices on their own reading and on subsequent events within the text itself. The result of this is that the student continually thinks laterally and considers the more interesting methods such as structure and voice, rather than micro analysis of bits of language. Contextual understanding is subtly applied to discussion and enhances the thread of argument - this can be seen in the application of Miller's writing and in the comment on the futility of hope for the lower classes in 1920's America. Both of these comments are fully integrated into discussion of the text rather than acting remotely as unconnected knowledge, they are also suitably brief and do not labour on ideas which sit outside of the text itself. The use of precise adjectives and adverbs such as 'doomed' and 'paltry' mean that analysis is effortless and sustained - perhaps seen best in the paragraph on Myrtle where discussion is perceptive and assured and the student offers sharp understanding of the narrative arc. Similarly in the paragraph on Gatsby and the green light, symbolism is discussed confidently and there is a range of excellent textual choices integrated into the argument to ensure that all ideas are fully pinned down in events within and across the text. This is a very good answer, clearly operating at the top of the mark scheme.

Printed in Great Britain
by Amazon